Why Can't My Child Behave?

of related interest

Reparenting the Child Who Hurts
A Guide to Healing Developmental Trauma and Attachments
Caroline Archer and Christine Gordon
Foreword by Gregory C. Keck, PhD
ISBN 978 1 84905 263 4
eISBN 978 0 85700 671 4

Foster Parenting Step-by-Step
How to Nurture the Traumatized Child and Overcome Conflict
Dr Kalyani Gopal
ISBN 978 1 84905 937 4
eISBN 978 0 85700 751 3

The Foster Parenting Manual
A Practical Guide to Creating a Loving, Safe and Stable Home
Dr John DeGarmo
Foreword by Mary Perdue
ISBN 978 1 84905 956 5
eISBN 978 0 85700 795 7

Life Story Work with Children Who Are Fostered or Adopted
Creative Ideas and Activities
Katie Wrench and Lesley Naylor
ISBN 978 1 84905 343 3
eISBN 978 0 85700 674 5

Creating Loving Attachments
Parenting with PACE to Nurture Confidence
and Security in the Troubled Child
Kim S. Golding and Daniel A. Hughes
ISBN 978 1 84905 227 6
eISBN 978 0 85700 470 3

Attaching in Adoption
Practical Tools for Today's Parents
Deborah D. Gray
ISBN 978 1 84905 890 2
eISBN 978 0 85700 606 6

Welcoming a New Brother or Sister through Adoption
Arleta James
Foreword by Gregory C. Keck, Ph.D
ISBN 978 1 84905 903 9
eISBN 978 0 85700 653 0

Why Can't My Child Behave?

Empathic Parenting Strategies that Work for Adoptive and Foster Families

Dr Amber Elliott

Foreword by Kim S. Golding

Jessica Kingsley *Publishers*
London and Philadelphia

Figure 2.1 from Beek and Schofield (2006) is reproduced with permission from BAAF.

First published in 2013
by Jessica Kingsley Publishers
73 Collier Street
London N1 9BE, UK
and
400 Market Street, Suite 400
Philadelphia, PA 19106, USA

www.jkp.com

Library of Congress Cataloging in Publication Data
Elliott, Amber.
  Why can't my child behave? : empathic parenting strategies that work for adoptive and foster families / Dr. Amber Elliott ; foreword by Kim S. Golding.
    pages cm
  Includes bibliographical references and index.
  ISBN 978-1-84905-339-6
  1. Problem children. 2. Foster children. 3. Adopted children. 4. Parenting. I. Title.
  HQ773.E45 2013
  649'.1--dc23

                              2013012294

British Library Cataloguing in Publication Data
A CIP catalogue record for this book is available from the British Library.

ISBN 978 1 84905 339 6
eISBN 978 0 85700 671 4

Printed and bound in Great Britain

Contents

Foreword

Within the western world there is a strong tradition of parenting based on social learning theory. This focuses the parents on using rewards and consequences to achieve acceptable behaviour in their children; parenting strategies such as time-out; praise, rewards and ignoring stem directly from this theory.

Children who have been developmentally traumatised by their early experience and are emotionally insecure as a consequence need very special parenting if they are to recover from their early experience. These children generally cope less well with this traditional parenting approach. A clear explanation of why these ideas are less helpful for this group of children and what parenting approach can provide a helpful alternative is therefore very welcome. In providing this, Amber Elliott has also provided us with an approach to parenting children which is likely to benefit all children, whether secure or insecure. It is time our ideas about parenting our children are based as much on connecting emotionally with them as they are about managing the behaviours that are so often an expression of this emotional experience. This book will move us in that direction.

I remember being introduced to behaviourism, the school of psychology which led to social learning theory, as a young undergraduate student. The lecturer told us a story of a group of students who decided to play a trick on him. Unbeknown to the lecturer they looked attentive and interested when he stood on one side of the lecture theatre but bored and disinterested if he stood on the other side. The lecturer quickly started to deliver his lecture from the side which met with the interest. His behaviour changed because of the response it led to; social learning theory in action. It was a powerful example of the way that we can control the behaviour of another.

At the time I found this appealing; now I am much more cautious. If we use such social learning ideas with children we may well get the behaviour that we are seeking, but what are we losing along the way?

Children learn appropriate behaviour.

Children do not learn that they are loved unconditionally – I will love you no matter what.

Children do not discover that they can engage in reciprocal relationships of mutual influence – You can delight in me, I can delight in you.

Children do not experience a deep emotional connection with another – We can share positive emotion, you can support me with negative emotion.

If children are getting these experiences alongside 'behaviour management' then they will be emotionally healthy and the parents may have some strategies which get them through the tougher times. Social learning theory can provide some helpful ideas for parenting, but alongside an emotionally rich and supportive environment.

What of the child whose early experience has been abuse, neglect, instability, loss and separation? These children do not know that they are loveable. These children find reciprocal relationship terrifying not delightful. These children fear emotional connection anticipating the hurt that seeking such connection will bring. Children become controlling instead; it feels safer and this safety is worth sacrificing relationship for.

Behavioural management based upon social learning theory; 'reward-punishment thinking' reinforces these controlling behaviours and moves the child even further away from reciprocal, emotionally connected relationship. As a consequence they cannot develop emotionally. They remain trapped in their early experience and in the deeply unsatisfying controlling relationships that feel safe but impoverished. Part of their humanity is lost along the way. This is a tragedy we cannot afford.

Empathic behaviour management offers an alternative, one that is essential for hurt children but will benefit all children everywhere. In this book Amber Elliott introduces the reader to empathic behaviour management and shows the importance of this to brain development and recovery from trauma as well as helping children behaviourally. Parents are encouraged to rethink behaviour within the context of meeting the emotional needs of the children. Understanding the experience which has led to the behaviour means that parents can empathically help their child to behave in a more acceptable way (correction) whilst maintaining a connection with them.

Secure children grow up knowing and believing in this connection. They know that they are loved unconditionally and that their parents are interested in their experience of the world. Thus when parents use correction; the children already feel connected. Secure children will modify their behaviour in line with the consequences provided by their parents without doubting the parents love and security.

Insecure children, lacking this security, are less likely to modify their behaviour in line with the parent's wishes. Instead they will behave in ways which help them to feel some increased sense of safety and security. This may or may not involve the parents. When parenting insecure children more attention needs to be given to connection before we can correct the children. Understanding the emotional experience of the child allows the parents to provide empathy for this experience whilst also providing some support for behavioural change. The parent connects before correcting, and ensures that they don't correct without good understanding. This is what is at the heart of this book; with clear explanations and lots of practical ideas Amber helpfully guides the reader through the use of empathic behaviour management and how to apply these ideas with a range of complex and challenging behaviours.

Social learning theory has provided us with a useful framework for raising our children based upon the logic of reward-punishment thinking. As these ideas have been embraced by parents social learning theorists have been at pains to ensure such approaches are used positively with an emphasis on positive relationships. However, despite this emphasis I hear daily about approaches being used with children that seem more focused on punishment than reward. This can only give rise to a generation of insecure children. I believe it is time to re-think our approach to parenting children and managing their behaviour. It is time that empathic behaviour management becomes part of our way of supporting all children; that we put connection with our children ahead of correction of their behaviour. Children will still be give boundaries and guidance; they will still learn the difference between acceptable and unacceptable behaviours. Importantly they will also be experiencing their emotional life being understood, valued and supported. They will be learning the value of reciprocal relationships and their instinctive need for connection with others will be met.

This approach to parenting children is based on what makes us most human; our capacity to connect with each other. This will not just reap rewards at the level of behaviour but will also ensure that children grow up to be healthy at the biological level.

Empathic behaviour management gives us the promise of raising emotionally healthy children. For children who have been raised initially within very challenging parenting environments; children who have experienced trauma within the relationships that are most important for them, empathic behaviour management is the only way forward. These children do not respond to reward-punishment thinking. This just reinforces their detachment from others. These children may initially fear the connection offered by empathic behaviour management. They will anticipate hurt and further loss. When parents stay with it however the children will over time regain the trust that they were born with but which was taken from them by the circumstances of their birth.

Children will learn that they are loved unconditionally.

Children will discover that they can engage in reciprocal relationships.

Children will experience a deep emotional connection with another.

This parenting approach will help children to recover from their early experience and to move towards adulthood as emotionally healthy young people able to fulfil their potential in every way.

Kim S. Golding
Clinical Psychologist

'I've Tried Everything! Why Isn't It Working?'

The long answer…

Being a parent is the most important job in the world. Parenting a child who doesn't know how to be parented is the most difficult job in the world. Doing it well, armed with the right information, can change not only the lives of the most vulnerable members of our society but also society itself.

Understanding what an awesome task foster carers and adopters have every day is the reason that I wanted to write this book. I have worked with many, many foster carers, adoptive parents and their children during my career. In my work I've learned an enormous amount from academics and the emerging research on this topic but also from carers and children themselves.

Until recently there really wasn't much scientific information available about the best way to help children who have suffered abuse and neglect. The fantastic news is that it is available now. However, there is still a great deal of work to be done to make sense of the science and turn it into strategies that make a difference.

In the absence of the inspiring scientific understandings that are now available, most foster carers and adopters manage their children's behaviour in the best way they know. Most carers, parents and professionals have been trained to deal with the difficult behaviour of abused and neglected children using the same approach as would be used with any other child; that is, to use what will be called throughout the book 'reward-punishment thinking' (the theory that behaviour change is most effectively created by rewarding desired behaviour and punishing unwanted behaviour).

Carers and professionals have been influenced for a long time by attachment theory (the understanding of the importance of an infant's relationship with their primary caregiver to the child's future emotional well-being and mental health). It seems to be wonderfully integral to the theoretical training of foster carers and social workers involved in fostering and adoption. However, in my experience, professionals (including foster carers) and adoptive parents often run out of attachment theory-based ideas when it comes to the 'here and now' difficulties of managing the challenging behaviour of their children.

A couple of clarifications

Before getting into thinking about what is useful to change and how, I'd like to clarify a few things. First, this book is specifically written for fostered and adopted children who have experienced some degree of early trauma (which, in my experience, is 99.9% of fostered and adopted children). However, the principles, science and strategies apply to all children.

Second, the term 'carers' is used throughout the book. This is used as shorthand for anyone parenting developmentally traumatised children, i.e. foster carers, adoptive parents, residential home staff, etc.

Finally, the word 'trauma': when trauma is referred to it refers to what researchers have called 'developmental trauma' (van der Kolk 2005) or 'relational trauma' (Schore 1994). This is different to the trauma contained within diagnoses such as 'post-traumatic stress disorder' (PTSD) in relation to war veterans, or as a result of car accidents, or the type of trauma that might be discussed in casual everyday conversations.

PTSD is commonly the result of a one-off, life-threatening event that causes flashbacks, intrusive thoughts, nightmares, and often a multitude of other difficulties. PTSD disrupts the ability of a functioning person to cope; developmental trauma, on the other hand, severely alters (and in some cases prevents) the *development* of the *capacity* to cope.

The profound impact of developmental trauma explains why the challenge for foster carers and adopters is so great and why behaviour management strategies just don't cut it with developmentally traumatised children. The behaviour seen in these children as 'naughty' or 'challenging' is frequently an expression of a child's survival strategies and therefore their disrupted personality and brain development. Amazingly, though, in the majority of cases these effects are reversible but only if the right logic is used to inform the strategies that are employed.

The importance of getting it right

In addition to carers' passionate motivation to care for traumatised children because they want to make a difference in their lives, there are some compelling statistics about the importance of this care too.

More than half of all children in the care system have chronic and disabling mental health problems (Blower *et al.* 2004; Dimigen *et al.* 1999; McCann *et al.* 1996); compare that with 10 per cent of children that aren't in the care system (Meltzer *et al.* 2003). These figures are staggering to see on paper but I'm guessing that they might not be news to carers.

What might be new information, however, is that the *most* important people in making a difference to these traumatised children are not therapists, psychologists or social workers (though the right input and support from these people can be crucial) but you, the person who has day to day, intimate care of these children. Most of the valuable work that other professionals offer can only be done through you. Put simply, this is because these children's problems have been caused by bad early relationships with primary caregivers, and so the only way of dealing with the problems is via a good parental relationship later in childhood. A positive parental relationship is crucial and in combination with the right mind-set and strategies it can, in some cases, be enough to make the difference for these children.

Often children traumatised by abuse and/or neglect also need help from other professionals, though for many of them the right therapeutic parenting techniques will be enough. Regardless of who else is involved, carers are crucially important and they will still have to deal with the everyday parenting challenges. Using these techniques will help carers to be part of the therapeutic solution for their children.

It's no wonder, then, looking at the mental health outcomes for traumatised children, that their emotional turmoil can often transform into challenging behaviour. In order to effectively build a good relationship and do anything transformative for traumatised children it is crucial to understand this behaviour as an expression of trauma rather than as naughtiness.

The travesty for these children is that, all too often, the right messages fail to make it through to the people looking after them and the wrong strategies can make things worse for them. For example, 'The naughty step', which is a version of time-out (the enforced exclusion of a child from interaction with other people; a form of extreme ignoring of 'bad' behaviour), is the method parents and carers are told repeatedly to use and it has become part of common parlance. However, when children's trauma is the focus, the idea of dealing with the challenging behaviour of a child whose understanding of parenting and relationships is marked by neglect, unavailability and abandonment, by sending them away and insisting that they are isolated, i.e. replicating and reminding them of their past neglect, really isn't right.

It's likely that the vast majority of carers will, at some point, have used time-out with their child and that is completely understandable. There is huge pressure on carers not only to manage behaviour assertively, but also to *be seen* to manage behaviour assertively. Strategies such as time-out also make perfect sense when using reward-punishment thinking. Thanks to new understandings, however, there are now other, more scientifically sound, options for developmentally traumatised children.

Box 1.1 describes a typical dilemma faced by traumatised children and their carers. The theoretical topics that I discussed with Simon and Rachel are crucial in helping carers to develop the new logic. These are the topics that I'll go on to explain later in this chapter.

Box 1.1 'Her behaviour just isn't logical!' – developing a new logic

Simon and Rachel were two long-term foster carers who came to me when they were really struggling with their long-term foster child, Sarah, who was seven. The difficulty was that Sarah often had explosive outbursts of rage, during which she would scream, shout, cry and hit out at her carers. She would also accuse Simon and Rachel of being unfair to her. These outbursts came without an apparent trigger.

Simon explained their dilemma in managing Sarah's behaviour by frustratedly exclaiming 'Her behaviour just isn't logical!' They had tried everything they knew: ignoring Sarah, sending her to her room and arguing with her flawed accusations of unfair treatment.

Simon and Rachel were having serious doubts about whether they could continue to care for Sarah because they felt that her behaviour was not responding to their (good) parenting.

I spent time with this family helping them to understand that they were right, Sarah's behaviour certainly was not logical using 'reward-punishment' logic but that it was, in fact, very sensible once we had a good understanding of the right logic.

We then spent time exploring this 'new logic' and using it to help Simon and Rachel to view Sarah's behaviour as if through 'new logic glasses'. We talked about emotional regulation, the effect of experience on brain and biology, trauma memory and shame. This new logic helped them to make sense of Sarah's behaviour and thus change their way of managing her rage outbursts. The process gave them much greater satisfaction in their parenting and their relationship with Sarah. By the end of the work, though they still had some very stressful and challenging times, there wasn't anything in the world that would have made them give Sarah up.

What's wrong with reward-punishment strategies?: 'old logic glasses'

Until the recent neuroscientific research was available, the best science available to tell professionals and carers how to understand and what to do with the behaviour of developmentally traumatised children was the same as was available for all children. Psychologists know this as behavioural theory.

This is the theory that most common parenting strategies come from, including praise, star charts, time-out, ignoring 'bad' behaviour, grounding, withdrawing privileges (e.g. TV, computer consoles; Box 1.2). Anything that involves rewarding or punishing a child's behaviour originates from behavioural theory.

This way of thinking is so commonplace that it has become quite difficult for most people to think of any parenting strategies or techniques that don't use reward-punishment thinking.

Box 1.2 Words associated with reward-punishment thinking and approaches

- Rewards.
- Punishment.
- Time-out.
- Ignoring.
- Praise.
- Sanctions.
- Consequences.
- Grounding.
- Boundaries.

Foster carers and adopters often ask why, when they're following the 'old logic' to the letter (Figure 1.1), they are struggling to manage their child's behaviour. Often carers seem to learn from experience that these methods are rarely effective with developmentally traumatised children.

Figure 1.1 Old logic/Black box theory/Reward-punishment thinking

Reward-punishment thinking assumes that it doesn't matter what is inside the 'black box' of a child's mind, the results will always be the same (Figure 1.2). However, the development of a good attachment relationship, that will equip a child with the abilities to thrive, relies upon an emotional connection with an attuned adult (i.e. an adult who is able to read, interpret and understand the inner world of the child) (Figure 1.3).

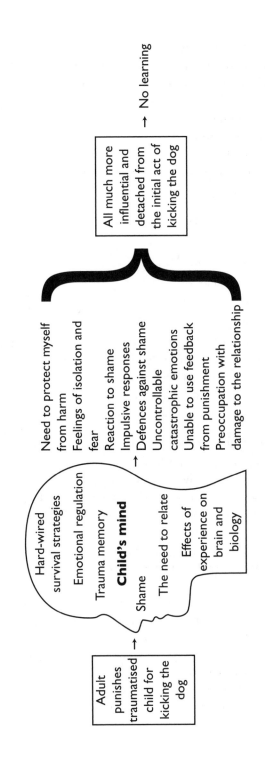

Figure 1.2 The effect of using reward-punishment thinking with developmentally traumatised children

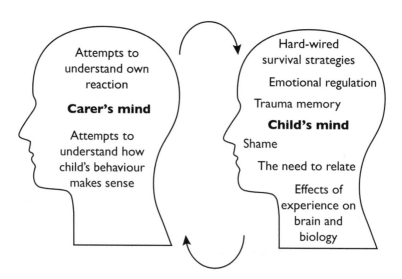

Figure 1.3 Empathic behaviour management model

As previously discussed, the development and functioning of the brain of a child who has been traumatised by abuse and/or neglect has had to be very different to a child who hasn't had these experiences. Human infants have a fundamental need to relate to another person. In most traumatised children this need has been thwarted through their negative experience of their primary carer(s) and the consequent impact on the infant's brain development. As a result the contents of the 'black box' are different from in other children. It becomes filled with the effects of their trauma, the strategies that have helped them to survive their experiences so far. The skills that developmentally traumatised children lack are typically those upon which reward-punishment thinking relies (Box 1.3).

If the survival strategies of traumatised children which, when viewed through the old logic glasses, look like attention-seeking, naughtiness, 'challenging behaviour', etc., are responded to with reward-punishment thinking, carers end up trying to train their children out of the drive to keep themselves safe. It's like training a child not to try to swim when they are drowning. Treatment of any act of survival, which does not take into account the necessity to survive, will cause damage to children's mental health and be very unlikely to succeed in changing their behaviour.

Box 1.3 Abilities and skills needed in order to learn from reward-punishment strategies

(The thoughts in quotation marks are more like unconscious ideas rather than children's conscious thoughts.)

- Cause-effect thinking, e.g. 'If I put my school uniform away I'll get a star on my star chart.'
- Ability to inhibit impulses, e.g. some gap (time to think) between a child's urge to steal and actually doing it.
- A strong belief (based on early experience) that love and safety is constant, unconditional and will not be removed permanently, e.g. 'If my carer/parent is angry with me now it doesn't mean she'll stop loving me.' 'If my carer stops me from watching TV tonight it's not because I'm horrible and unlovable; it's because I've done something that she doesn't want me to do again.'
- The ability to plan a resolution to the problem, e.g. 'I know he's annoyed with me now but later I could say sorry and then I know we'll be on good terms again.'
- The ability to regulate their own stress/emotion; in the midst of enormous anger and upset the child still has an underlying belief that they will feel OK again, e.g. 'I can cope with this.'
- Tolerance of shame, e.g. 'If my parent/carer is annoyed/angry with me I know that it won't last forever. She knows I'm a good person at heart.'

The reliance upon reward-punishment thinking also makes carers and other professionals focus on behaviour and leave them blind to the powerful emotional dynamics that abused and/or neglected children bring into their relationships. Using the old logic glasses therefore invites carers to act on their emotional impulses, which are often based on the child's implicit expectations about what relationships are like, and can often invite carers to replicate the child's past experiences (see Box 1.4).

Box 1.4 The invitations to replicate children's past relationships
Birth family experience

The birth parent rarely interacts with the child. The child develops a strategy of loudness (e.g. shouting, trouble making, aggression), which cannot be ignored, in order to demand attention.

Foster/Adoptive family experience

The child uses the strategy of demanding attention via loudness (e.g. shouting, trouble making, aggression). The carer feels controlled so backs off and/or carer follows the old logic and uses the 'ignoring "bad" behaviour' technique.

RESULT: The child has unconsciously invited the carer to ignore them. The carer has accepted the invitation.

Alternatively, in more extreme circumstances…

Birth family experience

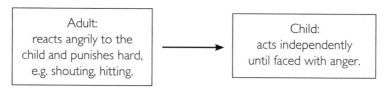

The birth parent reacts angrily to the child. The child develops a strategy of remaining largely self-reliant and avoiding their parent until they are faced with anger in the form of aggression or nastiness.

Foster/Adoptive family experience

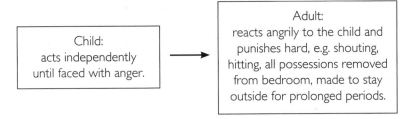

Child:
acts independently
until faced with anger.

Adult:
reacts angrily to the child and
punishes hard, e.g. shouting,
hitting, all possessions removed
from bedroom, made to stay
outside for prolonged periods.

The child uses the strategy of remaining self-reliant, e.g. putting themselves in danger, fighting their battles, etc. until faced with anger. The carer feels frustrated and eventually angry at the child's lack of response to more gentle techniques, so escalates their 'behaviour management', follows the old logic and uses more and more extreme punishments.

RESULT: The child unconsciously invited the carer to treat them harshly. The carer has accepted the invitation.

Traumatised children will unconsciously invite their carers into strategies that they understand even if they are aversive. Their behaviour therefore replicates, in carers, the child's birth family experience (Box 1.4). Chapter 2 contains more exploration of this issue and what carers can do to recognise and decline the invitation.

So why are the 'old logic glasses' so commonly used?

It is common that carers are exposed to many different professionals who advocate for the use of reward-punishment strategies with their developmentally traumatised child. Even if this hasn't been the case it is likely that most people will have heard them advocated in popular culture and society, e.g. TV programmes, in schools.

It is, consequently, very difficult to believe that a different approach could be more effective. The next few sections will explore why the old logic is so widely used and look at the scientific reasons why approaches based on new understandings are more appropriate for developmentally traumatised children.

The simplest explanation as to why reward-punishment thinking is still so widely used with developmentally traumatised children, despite scientific evidence of more appropriate ways, is that the science is still relatively new. The first persuasive neuroscientific evidence started to emerge in the 1990s and 2000s; indeed the 2000s has been dubbed 'the decade of the brain'. Whilst this may seem to be quite a long time, it takes a phenomenally long time to translate research into practice. This, typically sluggish, process of change is particularly slow in this case because reward-punishment thinking is so commonplace in westernised and more religiously structured cultures. It is also very challenging to move away from reward-punishment thinking with our children because it satisfies so many psychological impulses in those who use it, including those which have developed from our own experience of being parented, and is, therefore, intuitive in many ways.

All people have an inbuilt sense of justice and fairness. They also have a primitive, evolutionarily programmed reaction to anger and aggression. Looking after developmentally traumatised children means living with someone who might treat their carers aggressively, unfairly and/or unpredictably and may be unable to be apologetic. Of course, no child treats adults entirely fairly, they need more from an adult than an adult needs from them, but a child traumatised by abuse and/or neglect often presses more of those buttons than other children do.

It is perfectly logical therefore that, when a child is aggressive towards their carer, implicitly criticises them by not accepting their parenting or in other ways treats them unfairly, carers will feel somewhat hostile to their child. There would be something wrong with a person's self-esteem if they felt unmoved by such treatment. I certainly experience a broad range of emotions (affection, disgust and anger being just a few) about the children with whom I work and, contrary to what we're 'meant' to feel, often, these emotions are negative.

Acknowledging and understanding these feelings can be crucially important in understanding a traumatised child but also in helping carers not to react to the child in ways that won't be helpful, though they might feel very satisfying. Reward-punishment thinking enables carers to react, without needing to understand the underlying cause of behaviour, whilst also appealing to senses of justice and retribution. However, this reaction enables carers to disregard information about whether the strategy is effective in preventing the behaviour from occurring on another occasion.

The science behind the 'new logic glasses'

Fundamentally, traumatised children have missed out (to greater and lesser degrees) on the processes that enable children to develop the skills that they need in order to learn from reward-punishment thinking (listed in Figure 1.2). Such children are consequently immature in their ability to deal with relationships in general, let alone the challenging aspects of relationships, that is, when they might fall out with their parents or carers. Of course, children will vary greatly in their development of these skills. Some may have had some good enough experiences and so may have been able to develop some of the skills.

Many carers will have heard of the 'nature/nurture debate'. It's been an important talking point in parenting for decades about whether our biology (nature) or our experiences (nurture) are most influential in shaping our personalities. Recently, neuropsychological research has revealed that our biology and experiences aren't actually two entirely separate domains. There are two areas of the 'nature' part of this debate that are particularly relevant to children traumatised by their early experience.

Genetics

Research is now revealing more and more about how early experience affects even something as (seemingly) purely biological as genetics. Scientists have been able to look at genes and observe how their expression, that is, whether genes are switched on or off, is impacted by experience.

In relation to our genes it is useful to think about our biological make-up as partly written in pen (DNA) and partly written in pencil, that is, parts of our genetic make-up are altered and adapted by our experience as babies (epigenetics). The pencil writing means that our genes can be strengthened, weakened or even turned off or on, depending on what is best for the environment into which a person is born (Miller 2012).

It might be useful to think of the difference between genetics (what is inherited from our parents) and epigenetics (the way genes change depending on our infant experience) using the analogy of playing a CD. The genetic information is like the CD itself but the way the CD sounds is dependent upon the settings used on the CD player. The bass can be turned up, the sound can come from the left or the right speaker and the CD can be muted altogether. Ultimately the CD (genetics) provides the fundamental parts of the music but the settings on the CD player (epigenetics) alter how it is heard in an organised and predictable way.

This means that babies' experience, as they develop through their foetal stage and into early childhood, actually changes which genes will be available to them throughout their lives. Some of this genetic information will even be passed on to the child's own children. As this type of research is brand new it is not yet clear whether gene expression can be changed back again by different experiences in later life. Whether or not the genes of our children that have been altered by experience can be changed back, it is certainly possible to change the emotional world of our children and therefore their brain function and the behaviour they display.

Brain development

Compared with other mammals, human babies are effectively born too early. This has allowed us as a species to evolve smaller pelvises so that we can stand on two legs and use our hands to be more productive. As a result of this evolutionary transformation a newborn baby's brain is only 25 per cent of its final size (as compared to 45% in baby chimpanzees) (Eccles 2005).

This means that babies have an awful lot of brain growth to do when they are out in the big, bad world. For our children the world, as they know it, has been bigger and badder than for most.

For many of our children even that first 25 per cent of their brain that has developed, in the womb, has done so in conditions that were far from ideal. Many babies are exposed to alcohol, drug use and violence, as well as excessive fear, depression and/or anxiety neurochemicals, even before they're born.

In order to develop healthy and well-functioning brains babies need sensitive care and a safe environment (this will be explored further, in the 'Emotional regulation' and 'Trauma memory' sections of this chapter).

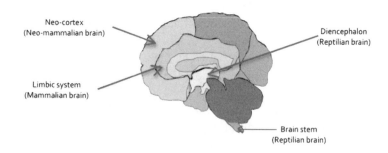

Figure 1.4 Relevant areas of the brain

The parts of the brain that suffer the most when a baby does not have these things are the pre-frontal cortex (right behind our foreheads) and the limbic system (the second layer of the brain) (Figure 1.4).

The pre-frontal cortex (sometimes referred to as the neo-mammalian brain), when we have one that works well, helps us to think about the future, understand cause and effect, have empathy and manage strong impulses and emotions. These sophisticated cognitive abilities are often called *executive functions*.

The limbic system (sometimes referred to as the mammalian brain) is where humans hold their ideas about relationships and emotional safety.

Astonishingly, there is also emerging evidence that even the development of the most primitive parts of a person's brain, the diencephalon and brain stem (sometimes referred to as the reptilian brain), are held back by early abuse and neglect. For example such basic functions as the ability to swallow may be seriously impaired in traumatised children (Perry 2011). When children have not had the opportunity to develop these areas of their brains they will struggle with even such fundamental things.

All of these areas of the brain are impacted by the stress hormone, cortisol. Cortisol is a perfectly typical neurochemical that everybody produces in times of stress and is, in most cases, harmless. However, the amounts that are produced in infants who are abused and/or neglected can be extremely toxic to their developing brains.

The good news is that, if these problems can be addressed before the age of three, it is possible to make a huge difference to children's brains quite quickly. After three years of age it is still possible to make an enormous difference to our children's brains by providing them with the experiences that they have missed out on. It is, however, often much slower as the brain has already become quite set in its ways by this point in its development. This is no reason for carers to lose heart about their older children though; if they use the right strategies it is entirely possible to make a very substantial difference to their lives.

When all this information starts to sink in then so does the idea that many traumatised children are stuck, in their emotional development, as babies or toddlers. In order to develop beyond these stages they literally have to develop new neural pathways. The child's experience of a loving relationship with their carer, as they use appropriate techniques, is the perfect combination with which to help the traumatised child.

Emotional regulation

Babies are born as chaotic bundles of emotion. For evidence of this just think carefully about what babies do and how they make most adults feel (you could try the 'baby's cry' exercise (Box 3.2 in Chapter 3). They cry like banshees about things that we, with our sophisticated understanding of the world and ability to cope with our emotions, don't even think twice about. Babies don't yet have adults' wonderfully masterful way of dealing with their external and internal worlds.

How do people develop this sanity-preserving skill (Figure 1.5)? It is developed after substantial experience of someone else managing the emotions first, in infancy. Babies internalise the reassurance and emotional coping skills of their carers. Until they can do this they borrow the skills, in fact the right frontal lobe of an attuned carer, a bit like an external hard drive might be used with a computer. This enables children to experience the full range of emotional intensity; their emotional thermostat is fully developed and goes all the way from 1 to 10.

Figure 1.5 Effective emotional regulation

In babies it is typical to see them developing their own emotional regulation strategies as they start to slowly separate from their primary caregiver (see Box 1.5).

Box 1.5 Typical emotional regulation strategies

- Thumb sucking.
- Sucking a dummy/pacifier.

- Holding a comfort blanket.
- Playing with their hair.
- Stroking their ear.

The majority of children who have been traumatised by abuse and/ or neglect lack the ability to manage their emotions to one degree or another and so their emotions are still, as emotions always are in babies, chaotic and overwhelming.

Children who are not enabled to develop emotional regulation skills can experience a limited range of emotional intensity, that is, their emotional thermostat is limited to either on or off, or perhaps they only have access to the 7 to 10 range (Figure 1.6).

Child experiences catastrophic anxiety and terror.

Child cries

Parent/Carer finds the baby's cry frightening/ punishing/ over-whelming etc.

Child continues to feel catastrophic anxiety and terror.

The adult cannot soothe and therefore communicates (verbally and non-verbally) that the feeling is indeed frightening and catastrophic.

Adult cannot cope with it.

Over time, when the child experiences this on *most* occasions, the child fails to develop capacity to regulate their own emotions.

Figure 1.6 Ineffective emotional regulation

As well as being a particular difficulty for developmentally traumatised children emotional regulation is a skill everybody loses from time to time. Box 1.6 demonstrates one such occasion in my life and the way that the empathy of someone else was my only way out.

Box 1.6 Emotional dysregulation and empathy

A few years ago I returned home from a week-long conference. I was lucky enough to be taking delivery of my new car on the day I returned. I was due to be back home by 7pm to meet the delivery man. Unfortunately, due to train strikes the train had not been able to deliver me to my home station, requiring me to walk for two and a half miles in the freezing November rain. This made me late; I'm not a fan of being late. It also made me cold; I'm even less of a fan of being cold.

I eventually arrived home and took problem-free delivery of my car before I got into the house. The heating had been off for a week; due to that and some ambitious redecoration work it was a most inhospitable place to come home to.

I sat down in my chilly home and then the realisation hit me; the next day was stuffed full with appointments and, although I had temporary insurance organised, I did not have any road tax on the car and no insurance cover note with which to get any.

I called my temporary insurers and explained the situation. Now, I would be lying if I tried to portray myself as the epitome of rational reasonableness by this stage. I was stressed, exhausted, hungry, cold and, frankly, grumpy. When speaking to the insurance agent I was polite but little more. She casually and off-handedly explained that there was nothing she could do at this late stage in the day and that I would have to speak with my permanent insurance company to see if they could do anything.

I dutifully called my permanent insurers, by this time a shade more anxious, stressed and grumpy than I had been with my previous company; let's be honest, I was a bit snappy. The woman I spoke with was rude in return and disinclined to help me. She said that there was nothing she could do and I was right in the first place, it was the temporary insurers who should be sending me my cover note.

By this point I was panicking and furious. I called the original company and didn't give the person on the other end of the phone much more than the chance to say hello; I ranted. I explained my situation, all of the phonecalls and how desperately important it was that I get a cover note. I eventually ran out of steam and there was a brief silence. Then came a calm, soft voice, 'Oh bless you, you've had an absolute nightmare, what a horrible experience, you must be so stressed. I'm sure I can get this sorted out quickly for you.' I crumbled; this young lad, who didn't know me or anything much about me, took all my over-the-top ranting, didn't get irritable with me in return, understood that I felt terrible and wanted to help.

The instinctive and, quite understandable, irritated, snappy, dismissive reactions of the two previous agents with whom I had spoken had served only to fire me up and make me even more incapable of getting my problem solved. This small gesture of empathy by the final agent, in the face of irrational and unfair treatment, got me instantly to a place of calm, pathetic gratitude, which enabled me to give him the information that he needed in order to help me.

One of the key strategies that will be described in the following chapters is *empathic commentary*. This strategy, which will be introduced in Chapter 3, is very useful in regulating children's emotions. The toilet training analogy (Box 1.7) may be helpful in understanding emotional regulation and why empathic commentary is so important.

Box 1.7 Understanding empathic commentary: toilet training analogy

Think about the process of toilet training a toddler.

At the beginning of the process the child will experience a sensation in their body that might make them wriggle around a bit and maybe grab at themselves. They have no concept that this uncomfortable feeling is indicative of the fact that they need to urinate.

Whilst toilet training, you, as the adult taking responsibility for the training, notice your child's behaviour, read what's going on in their body, via empathy, and then make the link between the child's sensation and what it means, for example, 'OK, I think you need a wee,' and then take them to the toilet or get the potty out.

In doing this you are empathising with the child's internal world, giving language to their abstract, subjective experience and providing them with a way of dealing with the internal problem.

In a multitude of different ways this is how attentive and empathic parents help babies to understand their internal world including their emotions. For example, a parent may read from their infant's body language that they are experiencing something; maybe the baby is focusing their attention over the parent's shoulder. The parent will interpret what the child is experiencing internally, for example, fascination with a moving light, and the parent conveys to the baby that their experience makes sense and that it is important, for example, the adult redirects their own gaze to the moving light and moves the child so they can see the light better; the adult will use an animated, smiley face and say something like 'Wow! That's shiny isn't it!'

Over time this repetitive process, of providing an adult mind as a mirror to the baby's own mind, teaches the infant what their internal world means, how it makes sense and therefore how they can communicate about it with others. It is this process that we are trying to replicate for developmentally traumatised children when we use empathic commentary.

Children who have not had the early experience of their primary caregivers regulating their emotions and understanding their inner worlds frequently appear as though disconnected from their internal states. These are the children who struggle to tell when they are hot or cold, or when they are hungry or full up.

Such children can also give the impression that their emotional expressions are in some way 'fake'. They have missed the experiences of emotional connectedness between themselves and their primary carers, that is, the experience of their emotional assertions has been disregarded. This has resulted in an internal separation of emotions and a sense of their legitimacy.

Traumatised children have a double whammy of emotional difficulty. Not only is their ability to manage their emotions compromised but they also have a tremendous amount of difficult emotions to deal with, far more than most children, indeed far more than most people.

It is no wonder then, that developmentally traumatised children have much greater difficulty in dealing with the relational challenge of being told off and other reward-punishment strategies. Using such strategies assumes that children can manage the emotional impact of disapproval, anger, excitement, etc. within their most crucial relationship. However, for most of our children this crucial relationship is also the one in which they are the most vulnerable. It is for this reason that the way in which carers manage the behaviour of a traumatised child is so much more important than reward-punishment thinking leads us to believe.

A traumatised child's experience of dispute, confrontation and conflict in their relationship with their carer is inherently stressful. For them to deal with this in a way that adults consider appropriate it requires them to submit to a more powerful person. It will evoke all of the shadowy, disembodied memories of their past experiences of these types of interactions with earlier carers. It also, therefore, provides wonderful opportunities to offer children an empathic understanding of their experience of stress in relationships and for them to experience alternative feelings, over extended periods of time, in such relationships.

Expecting a traumatised child to manage their emotions by themselves is, in most cases enormously unrealistic; it is the equivalent of expecting a child who has grown up in France to speak English when brought to the UK. Both skills feel instinctive when a person has them but are alienating and isolating expectations if they haven't.

Trauma memory

There are enormous misunderstandings about the way in which babies and young children 'remember' their experiences. For example, it is all too frequently said, in situations of children's exposure to domestic violence for example, something along the lines of 'well at least they weren't old enough to have known anything about it'.

This is an understandable idea but it is based on a misconception about human memory and as soon as the frightening, chaotic internal worlds of even well looked after babies become apparent, then this idea simply doesn't make sense.

Quite the opposite of being preserved from traumatic events, babies absorb these experiences not as events but as part of their reality and use them to develop their way of being. Babies have neither the ability to talk, nor even to think in an organised way using words. Their memories are stored in a non-verbal, procedural way. Think of babyhood as a time for learning how to 'do relationships' and, in fact, how to 'be a person', just as driving lessons are a time for learning how to drive. How to 'be' isn't something most people would be able to talk about or even consciously 'know' about, just as they couldn't talk accurately or coherently about the intricate sequence and pattern of subtle actions, reactions, thoughts, emotions, perceptions, sights, sounds and motivations needed to evade an overly confident cat on a busy, icy road. Even in adults, who otherwise have the ability to organise their experience using words, memories created in times of extreme stress cannot be stored in a way that enables them to be accessed verbally (Brewin, Dalgleish and Joseph 1996).

If this understanding of trauma memory is applied to a traumatised child it starts to become clear why their behaviour is very difficult for them consciously to understand and explain in terms of their past traumas. All of their abuse and/or neglect experiences *will* have been remembered but not necessarily in a way that they can access via words. Have a think about when you have smelled a perfume or heard a song that vividly brings back a memory that you didn't know you had, or a feeling that might have no context. The other day, for example, I somehow caught a whiff of something that reminded me of the very distinctive smell of Panini stickers (for those who don't know, these were collectable stickers that were very popular during my childhood in the UK). This sent me hurtling straight back to hoping for 'shinies' (metallic stickers) and the buzz of building up my collection. Much of the power of that memory is not accessible enough to me to describe it now, yet it was very emotionally provocative.

This aspect of the new logic should start to explain why emotional outbursts can seem to come without trigger and why reward-punishment thinking won't help carers to understand them. Carers can try imagining a traumatic, procedural memory flashback has popped into their child's mind. That intangible memory causes the child to have an explosive, aggressive outburst. The behaviour makes total sense as a reaction to the memory, though it doesn't make sense to the adults who are on the outside. Then imagine punishing or ignoring the behaviour whilst not attending to the trauma memory that caused it (as we would using reward-punishment thinking).

Using the new logic, punishing a child for an outburst triggered by a trauma memory or caused by the child's survival instincts makes as much sense as punishing them for flailing and trying to swim when they are out of their depth in ice cold water. The new logic will help carers to throw their children a life jacket (responsive strategies) and talk to them later about water safety (preventative strategies).

Shame

Most children haven't experienced neglect or abuse (thankfully) and so they can respond well to strategies based on reward-punishment thinking. These techniques work with these children because they understand that the person they care most about is thinking and feeling negatively about them, though only momentarily. This creates a little bit of shame in the child and to avoid this feeling the child will avoid the behaviour that created it in the future.

The effect of abuse and neglect on children is to give them an overdose of shame. Abuse and neglect are shaming for babies and young children because, unable to understand the social world or the minds of other people, all they have is themselves. They are 'egocentric'. So when they, unconsciously, try to make sense of the parenting they receive the only person that can possibly be in control, and therefore responsible, is themselves. Therefore babies can only interpret their experiences as their own fault; they are deserving of the treatment and are therefore ashamed of themselves for warranting such treatment.

Babies do not have any concept that other people have minds that are different to their own. If they did they might be able to understand that the responsibility for the treatment they receive is someone else's. Instead, infants digest the abusive treatment as simply another experience that helps them to make sense of the world. The abusive treatment is feedback about their worth. Everybody, including babies, experiences shame if they feel that they are deserving of disapproval, negative judgement and/or punishment from others.

These ideas can then be applied to traumatised children. When strategies based on reward-punishment thinking are used it creates a little bit of shame. Traumatised children are hypersensitive to shame (because they've been previously given an overdose of it). It's very easy for anybody to react defensively when they feel ashamed but for children who have had too much shame it is virtually impossible for them not to be defensive in some way or another when they are confronted with even small doses of shame that are inherent in being told off (see Box 1.8).

Box 1.8 Signs of children defending themselves from shame

To work out whether a child is defending against shame it is useful to consider if any of the following occur:

- the child saying 'Well I didn't even want the PlayStation anyway!' when you've taken it away from them as a punishment
- explosive outburst
- going blank/'into a bubble'
- living up to their 'shameful' reputation
- revelling in being 'bad'
- 'You don't love me!'
- 'You're always picking on me!'
- 'It's always my fault!'
- 'I didn't do anything!' (even though they know you saw them rip up all your birthday cards).

'But won't he think he can get away with murder if I don't put in boundaries?'

This is the question that carers and I often wrestle with when we're using *empathic behaviour management*. It's a tricky issue and it is a difficult issue to navigate through.

It is important to clarify that parenting using empathic behaviour management (EBM) does not mean parenting unassertively or not being in charge. All children including, perhaps especially, developmentally traumatised children need their carers to be calmly confident, warm, assertive and able to understand and implement what is best for their child. Often when carers or parents are not calmly and assertively in control then children will feel unsafe, anxious and need to take control for themselves.

This is when it is crucial for carers to remember that they're dealing with the needs of a child whose development is at different levels, i.e. their physical, social, emotional, sexual, relational and intellectual needs may all be at entirely different stages. Traumatised children are often stuck in the emotional and relational stage of an infant. In order for carers to understand which kind of logic they should use (i.e. reward-punishment thinking or empathic behaviour management) it is useful to think about the stage of development of the child that they are dealing with at any given time.

One of the most crucial stages to recognise in traumatised children is their 'baby mode', i.e. when they have regressed to the stage at which they missed out on the most crucial elements of their emotional and relational development.

If the child is emotionally all over the place; reacts in extreme ways; cannot be satisfied by logical means; is aggressive, verbally or physically to themselves or to other people; or responds in a bizarre way, they are likely to be in their 'baby mode'.

If they are somewhat calmer and able to speak (reasonably) fluently to their carers about why they, for example, shouldn't have to do the washing up, albeit they still might be upset, shouting and/or crying, then they are more likely to be in their 'older child mode'. In the case of the latter, reward-punishment thinking might just work. In some cases, though, using these strategies might cause regression to the child's 'baby mode'. This can be dealt with, if it happens, with EBM strategies. If carers are in any doubt about which emotional level their child is at then EBM strategies are the place to start.

Another way of thinking about the different uses for our old logic and new logic strategies is very carefully to differentiate what they are being used for. It's a well-rehearsed mantra, used by some parents and carers when using our old logic/reward-punishment thinking; 'I like you but I don't like your behaviour'. However, most of the times that it is used, the words may indeed be said, but the overriding message, non-verbally, is *not* about how much the child is liked but rather how angry the adult is with the child *and* their behaviour. Therefore the words and the actions are saying entirely contradictory things. A key part of EBM is learning the importance of how non-verbal communication is used and the ways in which it is more powerful than anything carers might say verbally.

If carers think about the two elements separately (first, 'I like you' and second, 'I don't like your behaviour') and they genuinely mean the elements then both elements must be conveyed simultaneously. It is important for carers to show honestly, at these moments, that they *do* like the child. This will be explored in response to specific behaviours in later chapters but, in short, empathy is the key. It's perfectly understandable, of course, for carers to find themselves in a situation when it is very hard for them to feel positively about their child. It is important, whilst carers try to regain their empathy, for them to be honest about the feelings that they have, for example, say as calmly as possible, 'I'm feeling a bit cross and worried at the moment because you hurt your brother but we'll sort it out and we can have cuddles later.'

The following chapters focus upon behaviours that are examples of behaviour deriving from trauma rather than age-appropriate boundary testing.

Put simply…

If in doubt about what level of ability these children have with which to manage reward-punishment thinking, the safest default position is to think as though the child is at their *youngest* stage and respond accordingly, that is, how would you respond if the baby personality in front of you was in a baby's body?

The behavioural strategies that are fine for babies are also fine for developmentally traumatised children. So, carers should express their love for their children, stick to regular routines, plan quality time, smile, laugh, play and have fun with their children.

You already know the answers!

Carers should ask themselves, if your baby was kicking and screaming would you shout at them, take away their rattle, leave them alone and expect them to calm down without your help?

It is far more likely that happy, healthy enough adults would be a bit worried that something is wrong with their baby. Once the physical things, hunger, change of nappy, illness, etc. had been eliminated, the most likely course of action would be to try to comfort the baby. The adult would speak to the baby with a soothing voice, even in the face of their screaming. They would hold the baby, rock them, touch their skin and use an empathic facial expression that mirrors their own and demonstrates to the baby that the adult understands that they are distressed and that they want to understand why.

All of these things that adults do so instinctively for babies are perfect for developmentally traumatised children. However, when you look at the 15-year-old boy in front of you, who is a foot taller than you and sprouting chin hair, through the 'old logic' glasses we turn to time-out, angry faces and taking away the PlayStation.

When looking at traumatised children carefully and calmly through the new logic glasses then suddenly it's the old logic that doesn't make sense (Box 1.9).

Box 1.9 Reward-punishment thinking strategies versus empathic behaviour management strategies

Strategies to avoid
'Old logic': reward-punishment thinking

- Time-out.
- Ignoring 'bad' behaviour.
- Praise.
- Shouting.
- Exclusion.
- 'Why did you do that?'

Strategies to use
'New logic': empathic behaviour management

- Sharing in the child's joy, sadness, excitement, anger, etc.
- Mirroring emotions in a calmed way.
- Reading the child's motivations.
- Making sense of challenging behaviour.
- Emotional, empathic commentary.
- Taking the initiative to repair the relationship (after falling out).

The short answer…

So, going back to the title of this chapter, 'I've tried everything! Why isn't it working?' the short answer is that invariably carers work extremely hard to help their children but often using a logic that doesn't really fit for traumatised children. Until recently the science that would have allowed the development of the right logic and the most effective strategies hasn't existed.

What is empathic behaviour management (EBM)?

The following chapters will take carers through some of the most common problems that foster carers and adopters ask for help with, looking through the 'new logic' glasses. My hope is that this book will help carers to refocus on the instincts that they have for babies and apply them to managing the emotions, and therefore the behaviours, of their child.

Each chapter will focus on one difficulty that carers often find tricky. Chapters offer a three-stage process for dealing with these challenges using the EBM model (see Figure 1.3).

Stage One: The problem will be explored in detail, giving examples and detailing what the common 'old logic' tells us and what the typical strategies using reward-punishment thinking would be.

Stage Two: The new scientific understandings to the problem will be applied to the problem behaviour using the EBM model (Figure 1.3). This will help to develop understanding of the nature of the problem, why it has occurred, why it creates the emotions that it often does in carers and their children and why the strategies that carers might have tried already may not have worked.

Stage Three: EBM strategies will be suggested that target the different elements of the EBM model. These include responsive and preventative EBM for carers and their children.

The next chapter focuses on traumatised children's biggest weapon in their fight to recover from their experience – their carer. The chapter will explore how carers can maintain empathy and why it is more than just self-indulgent for carers to look after themselves.

Box 1.10 Things to remember when using EBM

- Your child's behaviour is an expression of how they feel.
- Reward-punishment thinking often prevents carers and other professionals from seeking to understand and empathise.
- Developmentally traumatised children are unlikely to be able to tell their carers how they feel, or even know themselves.
- It is possible, although it often takes quite a lot of effort, to work out how the behaviour of developmentally traumatised children makes good sense and how it has been a pragmatic and/or adaptive strategy.
- In order to manage the behaviour of developmentally traumatised children it is crucial that we understand how they feel.
- Understanding the emotional cause of a behaviour will often render punishing the behaviour senselessly.
- To implement understanding and empathy carers should parent with warm, calm assertiveness.
- For carers, looking after themselves should not be thought of as self-indulgent. Children need their carers to be in good emotional shape in order to use the relationship to help them to recover from their experience.
- Carers' non-verbal communication with their children is more important than their verbal communication, i.e. what you say is not as important as the way you say it.
- Carers should watch out for signs that they are accepting children's invitations to replicate their earlier relationships (see Chapter 2).
- When using EBM carers will often see instant effects *but* they won't necessarily stick. It usually takes years of using these types of strategies to see results that last.

CHAPTER 2

The Importance of Carers' Emotions

'Why are we talking about me? Just tell me what to do with my child!'

One of the key needs of developmentally traumatised children is that the personalities and brains of these children are not able to cope well with things on their own. Traumatised children cope much better when they can do things with the support of another person who has their emotional state foremost in their mind, just as babies do.

The relationship with parental figures is so crucial for traumatised children that it is important to take a serious approach to understanding and looking after the emotions provoked in carers, before anything can be done about the emotions of their traumatised child. Incidentally this also applies to any professionals reading this.

Empathy is the key

First of all it's useful to make sure that we mean the same thing when we're talking about empathy. In this book, empathy doesn't necessarily mean feeling sorry for the traumatised child, although this may happen if there is an empathic connection. For the purposes of empathic behaviour management, empathy is about understanding what feelings another person is having; thus understanding their motivations, decision making, desires and behaviours. To really understand another person's feelings, rather than just make a reasoned guess, based on what they say and do (much as a computer could do), we have to genuinely feel a bit of what they are feeling. Looking back at Figures 1.4 and 1.5 in Chapter 1 might help with thinking about this.

Whilst steeped in evolutionary and neuroscientific relevance, moments of empathy are seemingly magical connections between two brains, which spark neurological connections in babies and bonds between people of all ages. Think of the last time someone you really care about sat and cried with you or told you some fabulously exciting news. The chances are that you shared their emotions and felt a little bit of what they felt. That process was empathy: two brains briefly connected and shared the same feeling and even the same neurochemicals.

Empathy, in this sense, is the reason that people cry at a weepy film or feel scared at a horror; it involves a willingness to lend the emotional part of our brain to the characters who convince us of their plight.

Of course everybody feels empathy for traumatised children, don't they? Frankly, the answer is often no. A lack of empathy for such children is not uncommon and it's not even the slightest bit surprising when the way that empathy works is understood, and how trauma in infant relationships affects empathy, not only in those early relationships, but in later relationships too.

The embodiment of trauma in traumatised children frequently means that feeling genuine empathy for them is very challenging. Children, indeed all people, tend only to behave in a way that invites empathy when they have an expectation that empathy is on the relationship menu.

Remaining empathic to developmentally traumatised children is an enormous challenge. Children come to carers with all of their horrific stories, thoughts and experiences. Yet, because these things were experienced in a cocoon of isolated childhood, in which their experiences were not critiqued or compared, children arrive not with all of their outrageous and horrific tales to tell but as an embodiment of their experiences. Children traumatised by abuse and neglect are not open books; we have to interpret and analyse the stories that inhabit them. The only possibility of doing this lies in finding ways to resist children's invitations to play familiarly negative characters in their story. To maintain enough attention, energy and compassion to do this, foster carers and adopters need to stay fresh and find ways to keep a firm grip on their empathy.

So, carers who have found themselves lacking in empathy for their traumatised child should certainly not judge themselves for it; it's a natural consequence of caring for the child's trauma. However, when carers want to introduce a new character into their child's story, and not take their invitation to stand in for the absent 'Mum' or 'Dad' character, then there are ways in which they can build their empathy reserves. Throughout the chapter (indeed the whole of the book) we'll deal with why maintaining empathy can be so hard, why negative feelings are so difficult to acknowledge, what the consequences of low levels of empathy are and strategies for developing and maintaining empathy for traumatised children.

Why empathy can be so difficult

Box 2.1 Why maintaining empathy for children traumatised by abuse can be surprisingly difficult

- It is very difficult to get a detailed history of children's lives and therefore to know what to feel empathic about.
- Traumatised children can behave in ways that are challenging to relationships. Although they were likely to have been good strategies for them in their abusive past they are likely to be useful in their new lives.
- Traumatised children's behaviour encourages us to evaluate and discipline rather than empathise.
- Exposure to information about traumatic experiences is exhausting and can lead to compassion fatigue.
- Carers' relationship expectations are likely to be different to those of the children they look after.
- It is very challenging to find someone to talk to who understands the difficult psychological processes inherent in looking after traumatised children, and with whom carers can be honest.
- Professionals tend to try to help carers and their children by using reward-punishment thinking with carers, which can have a deleterious effect on empathy.

'How do I know what I'm meant to be empathic about?'

An essential element in maintaining empathy for traumatised children is having accurate details about their history. It is consistently dismaying to hear stories of carers who receive children into their care accompanied by only the bare minimum of information about their experiences. Very often this is continued throughout placements, sometimes for many years. Carers are left to glean what they can from professional meetings and the questions they choose to ask. It is no wonder that carers struggle with sustaining empathy for their child's 'difficult' behaviour when they have no idea why the behaviour occurs and what they should be empathising with the child about.

In the absence of a good understanding of why a particular type of challenging behaviour occurs, it is entirely natural to default to the belief that the traumatised child simply needs the guidance and boundaries, via reward-punishment thinking, that are applied to all children.

Many carers are not provided with an accurate history of their child's life (for some, it seems that no adult knows their history in detail) but I would urge all carers, in the strongest possible terms, to ask, badger, plead and insist upon being given as much detail as possible about their child's history. It is then important to spend time listening, reading and understanding it. It is this history that helps all people working and living with traumatised children not only to maintain empathy but also to develop new logic on which parenting strategies can be based (see Box 2.2).

Box 2.2 The importance of having historical information
Part One

It's early evening on a busy weekday. Jocelyn is in the middle of preparing some dinner for her two children before she feeds the family cat, Bingo, and gets on with other household tasks. She's been away from home for the last few days seeing a relative and has returned just in time to pick the children up from school. She and the children have been home for an hour and the children have been playing on their games console, in between asking Jocelyn to mediate in minor disputes about what game they should play, resisting getting changed out of their uniform, asking about whether they can have snacks and what they'll be having for dinner.

Jocelyn has got some minced beef out of the fridge and is about to start chopping some vegetables when she hears an argument between the children, that has been bubbling away for the last few minutes, escalate into a full-blown shouting match. Jocelyn goes through to the lounge to resolve the dispute. When Jocelyn comes back into the kitchen she sees Bingo up on the kitchen work surface enthusiastically tucking into the pre-bolognaised mince. Jocelyn knows what a greedy boy Bingo can be so she shouts his name and rushes towards him clapping her hands to frighten him away from the food. Jocelyn chases Bingo out of the back door and then locks the cat-flap to stop him from coming in again. After a few minutes Bingo returns to the back door pining to come in. 'No, Bingo, you can stay out there; you've got to learn that you mustn't go near our food!'

What do you think about how Jocelyn handled the situation in relation to Bingo? What do you think Bingo learned from it? (Try to answer before you read on.)

Part Two

When Jocelyn's partner, Sam, comes home later that evening, after saying hello to Jocelyn and the children in the lounge, he goes into the kitchen to make cups of tea. From the lounge Jocelyn hears 'Oh, Bingo, there you are! I've been so worried! What on earth are you doing out there!' Sam opens the back door and lets Bingo in and gives him a big bowl of food. When Jocelyn comes into the kitchen she sees Bingo wolfing down his food at a rate of knots and asks what's going on. Sam explains that Bingo has been missing for the last two days.

What difference do you think the information about Bingo's absence makes to what he learned from his exclusion outside?

Do you think that Jocelyn would have done anything differently if she had known this extra piece of information from the start and if so why?

Whilst Jocelyn couldn't allow Bingo to eat the family's dinner she now understands that Bingo was behaving in an entirely understandable way. As a result of the understanding, and her consequent empathy for Bingo, Jocelyn no longer has any desire to punish him but wants to provide an environment that prevents Bingo's need to eat the family's food and understands that these were exceptional circumstances.

As many of the challenging behaviours of traumatised children are misdirected survival strategies they invariably need treating as though they are provoked by 'exceptional' circumstances, just like Bingo's indiscretion.

It is perhaps easy to assume that accessing the detailed histories of children who haven't been physically or sexually abused isn't that crucial but it can be even more important in cases of neglect. As mentioned in Chapter 1, babies' brains are negatively impacted by any prolonged absence of good enough care. Neglect is, in fact, the most detrimental thing for infants' brains; however, due to the nature of their experience, these are the children about whom we know the least.

Neglected children are less likely to have full medical records and parents are less likely to be able to give comprehensive accounts of their children's lives, therefore schools can often be the best sources of information about these children. In the absence of detailed information about neglected children, it is sensible to infer that they have suffered developmental trauma as a result of the neglect and that a tailored form of parenting is needed. The importance of adequate contextual and historical information cannot be overestimated in its power to inspire empathy; try the exercise in Box 2.3 to understand how.

Box 2.3 Empathy drives motivation to act

Take some time to consider and compare the following two scenarios.

Scenario One

Whilst watching the news on TV you see a story about the rise in the number of elderly people who live alone and are socially isolated. The programme makers have used library footage of an elderly woman making a cup of tea at home and they quote statistics about the rise.

Scenario Two

You have mistakenly received an item of mail that should have gone to your next door neighbour, June. June is in her eighties and lives alone. As you approach June's front door to post the letter through it you see June through the lounge window. She is sat in her floral, high-backed armchair. She appears to have her head in her hands. When you reach the front door you hear June's faint muffled sobs.

What is the emotional difference in the two scenarios?

Which scenario triggers most empathy in you?

Which scenario is most likely to alter your behaviour in relation to the social isolation of the elderly?

It is only when we can really feel the emotional power of someone else's heartache that we feel compelled to act. As I hope that you will have experienced in doing this brief exercise the key to staying motivated to act for traumatised children is to work to retain our empathy despite the challenges to it.

When children mirror the nastiness of their experience

Children who have been abused and neglected are shaped by their experience; they adapt their way of being to fit in with what they have had to deal with. They are often not easy children to look after or feel empathy for. Think of how vulnerable a trusting, angelic child would be in an abusive home; they simply would not survive.

As explored in Chapter 1, developmental trauma not only impacts on children's mental health but also the very fabric of their understanding of themselves, other people, the world and all of the inter-relationships between those factors.

Add to this the fact that humans are fundamentally social beings who respond to each other, not in a way that is entirely of their own design but in a responsive and reciprocal way. Humans tune into the person with whom they are interacting and respond based on their cues and how those cues map on to the individual's own history and understanding of relationships.

It is, therefore, no wonder that carers, looking after developmentally traumatised children, sometimes find it difficult to feel genuine empathy for their children and frequently find it difficult to sustain such empathy in the face of children's challenging behaviours.

I have worked with many carers who have had a child come into their home and their family, with character traits and behaviours that make feeling empathy for them very difficult. These difficulties range from overtly sexualised behaviours, for example, a seven-year-old girl sitting on a male carer's knee for a cuddle and then making eye-contact and rubbing her leg against the carer's groin, to a child who, much more subtly, gives a slight smile when a much-loved family dog is hurt, or simply a child who refuses to eat a meal that they had requested.

Carers frequently have experiences of their child's behaviour, similar to the ones listed above, without any knowledge of their history. Often, therefore, this means that they have little help in understanding how such behaviours may have been perfectly good and logical strategies for dealing with the early relationships that have shaped the development of their personalities.

The behaviours that children display as a result of their developmental trauma will have good reasons for being there; however, when viewed through the logic of reward-punishment thinking they frustrate, annoy, disgust and anger carers. This is a very difficult position from which to develop empathy.

Traumatised children will often display behaviours that are (unconscious) attempts to replicate the interactions they know and understand, no matter how terrible they may have been (see Box 1.4 in Chapter 1). These attempts present carers with social invitations to behave in certain ways. The invitations are just as subtle and just as strong as the invitation to queue rather than go to the front of the line or move to one side of the pavement when someone walks towards you. Our only hope of responding in a different way is to acknowledge how we are being invited to behave and that means being honest with ourselves regarding our feelings about the children we look after. These feelings are tremendously useful tools for understanding the internal worlds of our developmentally traumatised children.

The emotions of traumatised children are so powerful because they provoke equally strong emotions and responses in the adults around them.

Reacting to behaviour

Just as children instinctively behave in accordance with their previous experience, foster carers and adoptive parents instinctively respond to their children's invitations to join in with these types of interactions.

As a general principle it is useful to accept that out of character reactions to the behaviour of traumatised children are provoked, in some part, by the invitations traumatised children give us. There may also be many aspects of our own psychology that make reward-punishment thinking seem like logical responses to problem behaviours but such intuitive reactions may be detrimental to children's emotional development.

Understanding the origins of carers' feelings, when applying reward-punishment thinking to the behaviour of traumatised children, helps to make the adjustments needed to move towards strategies based on empathy for children's trauma.

The invitations implicit in any relationship tend to dictate carers' behaviour when reacting instinctively. However, pausing for thought in order to understand the intuitive reaction could help to devise more effective solutions.

Fundamentally, we all have an expectation of fairness and reciprocity (i.e. we expect that, to a certain extent, people will treat us as we treat them) and any breach of that social rule provokes negative feelings. Quite frankly, there would be something quite wrong with a person's self-respect if their instinct, in the face of rudeness, aggression and/or being ignored, wasn't anger, rudeness and ignoring, or some other form of reaction that conveyed how unhappy they are to be treated in that way.

In response to aggression, which will be explored in much greater detail in Chapter 4, animals have a physiological response that prepares our bodies to flee or to fight. It is evolutionarily programmed that, in the face of aggression, humans will frequently react aggressively. Unless, that is, they are able to notice and understand their own emotional reactions and the emotions of the children (in this case) that have provoked them.

Reacting aggressively to aggression satisfies a sense of justice and fairness and often feels quite intoxicating; it produces an adrenalin rush and provides the buzz of standing up for ourselves. Unfortunately, however, unless the person on the receiving end has some understanding of fairness and justice it will not help them to learn that their behaviour was unfair; indeed, it will be most likely to provoke an escalation of the problem.

How to deal with your negative feelings in the moment

Until it is possible for a carer genuinely to overcome the negative feelings that they may have about a child, by understanding the cause of their behaviour, it is very important for the carer to help the child to make sense of the emotional atmosphere between the two of them. What carers often do is deny that there is any problem with a 'No, don't worry, I'm fine.' However, emotions will always leak out via our non-verbal communication and so denying them simply causes more ambiguity and anxiety.

It is very important in interactions with developmentally traumatised children that non-verbal communication matches the verbal communication in emotional exchanges. Children who have spent their early months and/or years in emotionally volatile environments are very well trained to work out the emotional truth of what is going on, it will have been a skill that enabled them to protect themselves. These will be the children who, when there is any emotional ambiguity, feel the need to ask their carers persistently if they are OK or watch their movements like hawks.

One of the most useful strategies to deal with these tricky ruptures in the relationship between carers and their children is *emotional commentary*. Future chapters include details about the application of this technique to the challenging emotions and behaviours of your child, but it can also be applied to your own challenging emotional states. There are some examples of emotional commentary for carers in Box 2.4; try using them, applying the cautions that follow the box.

Box 2.4 Empathic commentary for carers' emotion

The following are examples of empathic commentary statements that you can use to help your child to understand the emotional rupture in your relationship with them before you can understand the origin and sense of their difficult behaviour.

- 'I'm feeling quite cross just now because you've smashed a window by kicking a ball when I told you not to. I will calm down in a while though.'
- 'I'm feeling quite upset with you at the moment because you shouted at me when I was trying to help you. Give me some time to feel better then we can talk about it.'
- 'Frankly, I feel very angry about what you just did to Josie. I'm going to try very hard to understand why you did that but it might take me a while to calm down.'
- 'I know you're trying hard. I'm just getting really frustrated because I can't get you to brush your teeth. I'll be OK again in a little while.'
- 'I'm so confused about why you're doing that. I will try to work it out though and we can have more of a chat about it later.'
- 'I've had a really bad day. I'm not cross with you, but I know you might think I am. I'll be fine once I've had a sit down and a cup of tea.'
- 'I'm feeling quite worried about Marie (foster mother) because the car's broken down but we'll work it out. I'm not cross with you though.'

It is important to take care not to slip into reward-punishment thinking and confuse emotional commentary with a technique for disciplining children. Remember that developmentally traumatised children are likely to react defensively to this type of shaming strategy (see Chapter 1). Therefore it is important not to exaggerate the feelings, nor use the commentary in a hostile way, and to try to be as calm as possible.

After there has been some explanation of a carer's emotional state to the child, it is useful for carers to take some time to work out precisely why they are feeling the way they are and/or the way in which the child's behaviour makes sense. When things are calmer carers can follow the issue up with their child and use some of the preventative strategies in the following chapters and/or commentate more accurately on the emotional states that caused rupture in the relationship.

Bear in mind that the time between the rupture and the repair of the relationship is likely to be very stressful for your child. They may persist in asking about what is wrong. Alternatively, they may anticipate such severe consequences, in relation to the rupture, that they may find a way to forget the fall-out between them and their carer and appear irritatingly blasé. In either case the child will need their carer to take the initiative to repair the rupture in the relationship, even if it appears that the child should be the one to apologise.

Another factor that can make it difficult for people to maintain empathy with developmentally traumatised children is repeated and prolonged exposure to details of trauma. When people are persistently exposed to horrific ideas that are painful to think about, it is not unusual to build up protective defences to prevent the assault of those awful emotions. If carers are not mindful of this tendency then it can make authentic empathy difficult to develop and sustain.

Compassion fatigue: 'I couldn't do what you've done!'

Many, many people find it incomprehensible to be in direct contact with the horror that abused and/or neglected children have suffered. Child abuse and its consequences create such powerful emotional responses in compassionate and caring people that even the *idea* of caring for such children often necessitates an exit strategy, that is, 'I couldn't do what you've done.'

Those people who do decide they can do it, particularly those people who decide to look after, and live full-time with, children traumatised by abuse and/or neglect, need other types of emotional exit strategies. Try the exercise in Box 2.5 to explore your experience of real empathy and how carers escape from it.

Box 2.5 Moments of empathy and how we escape

Think carefully about the last time you really felt deep empathy for your child, the last time that you actually experienced that gut-wrenching and horrific clarity about the real emotions, loss and catastrophe that your child has experienced. On the occasions when the protective fog lifts, it becomes painfully obvious why the effects of early trauma often take over to the detriment of the rest of life.

Whilst you're remembering the last moment of clarity try to think about what it would feel like to hold on to that feeling for any longer than a few minutes or hours.

- What would happen to you?
- Would you be able to go about your daily business?

- If you could, then how would that feeling impact on your day, the way you spoke with people and the way you perceived their actions and motivations?
- What do these feelings make you want to do?

In all likelihood you would have worked hard to get rid of those feelings about your child and quite right too! This strategy is testament to how good you are at emotionally recovering.

You might have tried some of the following strategies. Some of these thoughts are pretty hard to admit, even to yourself, but try to reflect carefully about which of these (or others) were your ways of getting away from the painful emotions evoked by truly, albeit fleetingly, empathising with your child. Make a note of which are most meaningful for you.

You might try:

- distraction, 'anything to take my mind off it'
- talking yourself out of the feeling
  - 'He was probably too young to have known what was going on.'
  - 'She's tough enough to cope with it.'
  - 'Maybe he deserved it.'
  - 'She must have encouraged it somehow.'

Please add your own if none of these quite fit…

No matter how people personally manage to escape from this experience, it should be possible to see that the temptation to do so can be irresistible. This does not happen because carers are cold and uncaring human beings, quite the opposite. If carers didn't feel their child's pain acutely they would have no need to resort to such extreme measures to avoid it.

The important part of this process is to acknowledge that the things that are said or thought in order to alleviate the pain are not necessarily accurate, for example, despite being ten months old he *did* know the violence was going on; she *was* a victim and not complicit in designing the abuse. Unless there is acknowledgement of the instinct to avoid painful empathy with traumatised children then it is not possible to begin to be able to tolerate enough of the children's pain to parent them constructively rather than in a way that alleviates adult discomfort.

Another crucial aspect of looking after children who have been traumatised by abuse and/or neglect is that, emotionally, they are operating at a much younger and, consequently, more needy stage of their emotional development. The level of emotional responsivity, attention, supervision and stimulation that they demand is much more akin to that of a baby rather than the older child that carers see in front of them.

When someone has a baby, they and others around them make tremendous adjustments to enable them to devote their time to that baby. They make enormous changes to their working life; they will often do little other than look after the baby's every need. If the new parent is lucky, people will bring them food so they don't have to spend precious time preparing and cooking a meal. Nobody bats an eyelid if they turn up at 3pm and finds the parent still in their dressing gown.

Looking after a developmentally traumatised child can be just as practically and emotionally exhausting as looking after a baby but society doesn't make anywhere near the same allowances. When carers start to give themselves credit for how demanding their job of looking after a developmentally traumatised child can be, they can begin to feel more able to alter their treatment of themselves and their child.

When two worlds collide

As well as considering the powerful dynamics that children bring to the relationship with their carers, it is also important to spend some time thinking about what carers bring to the relationship.

Everybody has had an experience of being parented, which has had a powerful impact on shaping their personalities and perspectives on relationships, in all their infinite and intricate detail. Everybody will have worked out, to one extent or another, what type of people they get on well with and what type they don't. It's uncommon however that carers get much of a meaningful chance to work out how well they will get on with their adopted or fostered child before they start living together. Often, the relationship expectations of the traumatised child will be very different to those of their carers. These relationship expectations can collide in a number of ways and can lead to misunderstandings and further disruptions in carers' ability to feel empathy for their child.

It is important for carers to understand their own ingrained ways of understanding relationships, most of which have been learned from their own experiences of being parented, as well as understanding their child's expectations of relationships. It is easy to assume that early experiences only need to be examined when there have been traumatic childhood experiences. However, there are so many subtleties and nuances in the formation of early relationships that it is unfortunately not as simple as defining them as traumatic and non-traumatic. Try using the questions in Box 2.6 to explore your implicit expectations of relationships.

Box 2.6 Understanding differences in relationship expectations

Scenario One

James and Carrie are a couple who have lived together for two years. They don't have any children, they both work and they share the household chores fairly evenly.

On a particular Wednesday evening it is James' turn to cook the evening meal. He's had a horrible day at work. Earlier in the week a project that James had been working on had gone wrong and his boss had blamed him for it. Carrie has also had a tough day. She had a telephone call earlier in the day to say that her auntie is unwell and Carrie is very worried about her. She has also been doing more than her fair share of the household tasks for the last week because James has been struggling so much with work.

When Carrie comes home at 7:30pm she finds James sitting in the lounge watching TV with no signs of any dinner being cooked.

Carrie is furious and makes sure James knows it. James argues back just as forcefully. They both defend their positions.

- Who do you think has the most legitimate grievance?
- What do you think James should do?
- What do you think Carrie should do?
- How would you have done things differently in James and Carrie's positions?

Scenario Two

Patsy and Farida have been friends for five years. Their youngest children go to the same primary school, they often socialise together, and they have shared good times and bad. They are each other's first port of call when they have troubles or when they are in need of a shoulder to cry on.

On a rainy Saturday afternoon the friends are out shopping together for school shoes for their children. Patsy finds a perfect pair of shoes and some trainers for her son Anthony but when she goes to pay for them her card is declined. She is embarrassed and asks Farida whether she could get the shoes on her card. Patsy assures Farida that she will pay her back as soon as she possibly can. Farida is happy to lend Patsy the money.

A week later the women meet as usual at the school gates; there has been no mention of the money and Farida is starting to worry about getting the money back. She will need to get some groceries at the end of the week. Farida mentions the money to Patsy and asks Patsy if she knows when she will be able to let her have the money back. Patsy looks taken aback and appears to be a little embarrassed and annoyed. She thinks, 'She knew I wouldn't be able to give it back to her this quickly!'

- Who do you think has the most legitimate grievance?
- What do you think Patsy should do?
- What do you think Farida should do?
- How would you have done things differently in Patsy's and Farida's positions?

Try the scenarios out with a range of people who have had different life expectations to you, without tipping them off as to what you thought. Compare responses and see whether there is a range of options on these issues.

It is likely that your responses and those that you have collected will have been shaped by each person's own experiences and consequent expectations of relationships. Some people may have particular ideas about gender roles of the importance of routines and therefore what is expected of James and Carrie. Some may have particular views about lending money, friendship and communication and so may respond in various ways to Patsy and Farida's story. The enormous range and variety of relationship expectations and assumptions means that what seems obvious and 'normal' in relationships to a carer may be strange, alienating and/or odd to a child with different experiences and expectations.

I'm guessing that Box 2.6 raised a few different perspectives on some very simple scenarios. I hope this will help to demonstrate how different relationship expectations and assumptions can be. Developmentally traumatised children, having had some extreme experiences of building relationships, may well have extraordinarily different expectations of relationships from their carers.

If carers of children traumatised by abuse and/or neglect arm themselves with a good understanding of their own history and how this has created their relationship expectations, particularly parenting relationships, then it will help them to reflect on the relationship misalignments when they occur. Try using Box 2.7 to explore the relationship expectations of carers and their children.

Box 2.7 The relationship expectations of you and your child

Fill in the chart below with your expectations about these topics and what you can guess, from your knowledge of your child and their experience, your child's expectations might be.

It can sometimes be challenging to think explicitly about our own expectations, as they are so well embedded within us, so it might help to talk them through with someone you trust.

	Your expectations	Your child's expectations
How should families interact around food?		
What should bedtimes be like?		
How should adults show affection to each other?		
How should adults and children show affection to each other?		
How should parent figures and schools interact?		
How should parent figures and children interact around the subject of sex?		
What should celebrations be like?		
What do people do when they are in a bad mood?		

What do people do when they're excited?		
How do adults deal with disagreements?		
What things should be private?		
Who should people talk to about private things?		

As well as carers' relationship expectations, that come from their experience of being parented, it is also important to think specifically about what carers expectations of their child were, before they arrived. It might be useful to use Box 2.8 to help explore these expectations.

Box 2.8 Your ideas about your child before they arrived

Before you do this exercise take some time to focus on what your life was like before you first met your child. Was your home decorated in the same way? How old were you, did the same people live in your home, did you have the same pets, etc.?

It might feel tempting just to say that you don't know in response to these questions but try to imagine and get into your earlier mind-set.

Why did you decide to adopt or foster? (your child in particular, if you can answer this)	
What did you imagine they would look like?	
What did you think your first meeting would be like?	
How did you think you would feel about your child?	

How did you think that they would interact with the rest of the people in your home?	
What did you think they would bring to your life?	
How did you expect your daily life would change?	
What did you think the positives of living with your child would be?	
What did you think would be difficult about living with your child?	
What did you think your relationship with your child would be like in the first couple of months of living with them?	
How did you think your relationship with your child would change over time?	
What did you think your child would get from being parented by you?	
Any other expectations you had before your child arrived?	

Fighting the horror of the emotional worlds of traumatised children, that is, the world that carers need to try to understand and empathise with, can be truly exhausting. It's important therefore for carers to give the parts of their brain that are working hard on being empathic plenty of rest, otherwise it becomes much more difficult to resist the urge to escape from the traumatic emotions of their children by abandoning their empathy.

Box 2.9 Nurturing your empathic brain

The concept of 'PIES' may be helpful as a checklist of personal well-being:

Physical: self-care, sports, physical activities, eating, sleep, relaxation

Intellectual: thinking and learning, ideas and stimulation

Emotional: being in touch with feelings, and being able to talk about them

Support: practical, financial, emotional, feeling understood and accepted

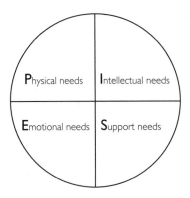

PIES

How do you look after yourself?

Think about four dimensions of yourself (PIES) and write down the activities that work for you.

Each person will have different things in their PIES and sections will vary in size depending on our interests, personalities and circumstances. Our PIES might also change over time.

Your support

Once carers have started to understand their inner worlds, and those of their children, they can use that as the foundation for recognising ruptures in empathy when they occur. However, even the most reflective people aren't particularly good at applying such rational ideas when under pressure, especially when we're learning and trying out a new strategy.

A crucial part of enabling carers to maintain empathic feelings for their children, who frequently behave as if they are not deserving of empathy, is maintaining a chain of empathy for themselves. Any foster carer or adopter needs to work at developing a non-judgemental, empathic support system. Family, friends, other carers and adopters, and professional support teams are crucial in this.

It is important for carers to have a third person (or even a fourth and fifth person) that they can trust, and talk honestly to, about the times when empathy has waned. This 'empathic buddy' could be a friend, a partner or anyone else that an individual carer feels that they can trust; although it really needs to be someone who isn't subject to the same relationship pressures as them, that is, someone who does not live with the child. Foster carers can ask their supervising social worker for this kind of support. However, it is very important for carers to be the judge of who their 'empathic buddy' should be.

The relationship needs to feel safe enough for the carer to be able to take the huge risk of being honest about the feelings that they have about their child in good times and bad. The person, or people, that a carer chooses to confide in needs to be able to understand, and believe, that the carer has the best intentions in relation to their child but that they will sometimes get it wrong. The empathic buddy needs to be non-judgemental about the inevitable breaks in empathy between carer and child, and the frustrated, angry comments that carers might make about their child. The empathic buddy also needs to be able to notice and tell the carer when these things appear to be happening and not make the carer feel terrible for it. It might be useful for carers to encourage their empathic buddy to read the first two chapters of this book to help them to understand what they are being asked to do and why.

Carers, in turn, need to be bravely honest and really talk about the difficult feelings they have and the times when they haven't been very empathic. It's also important that carers try to hear when their empathic buddy is telling the carer when they have noticed that empathy has faded.

Why is damaged empathy so difficult to acknowledge?
'Compassionate people are good people': professional narratives
There are many pressures on everybody who interacts with developmentally traumatised children to feel and behave in certain

ways. There is a dominant belief that having negative feelings about traumatised children means that carers are, at best, unprofessional and, at worst, terrible human beings. This is an example of how reward-punishment thinking is routinely applied to adults as well as children. It has implanted itself into our thinking as the only way to get people to change their behaviour. The thinking, so ingrained that it has become second nature, seems to be motivated by thoughts along the lines of, 'If I disapprove of the way that they are feeling then they are less likely to feel that way', or conversely, 'If I listen and empathise about this person's negative feelings I might encourage them to feel that way more often.' Unfortunately, this is a huge oversimplification of the importance of the emotions of foster carers and adopters, and the emotions of traumatised children.

Emotions are a fundamental part of being human and our best hope is to acknowledge them, try to understand where they came from and do our best to limit their negative impact on our behaviour. Just as it is harmful to control, condemn and punish the feelings of children, it is equally damaging for carers to do those things to their own feelings.

It is nonsensical, and psychologically harmful, for carers to judge and punish themselves for their emotions. It is really only the behaviours that emotions can lead to that can be justifiably judged. However, when the emotions that drive problematic behaviours are properly understood their punishment usually makes less sense. Typically conversations such as this, with adults looking after developmentally traumatised children, seem to go through the three-stage process that is detailed in the consultation with Gloria in Box 2.10.

Box 2.10 The very difficult process of acknowledging negative feelings about children

Gloria has come for a psychological consultation to speak to me about her foster child, Michael. On two occasions Michael has been found to have taken Jasper, the family dog, into his bedroom and seems to have been hurting Jasper by pulling out tufts of his hair. Gloria has spoken very quickly, in quite a loud, forceful voice. When she was talking about the specifics of what Michael had done to Jasper her upper lip curled with her mouth slightly open and she furrowed her brow and clenched her jaw. Gloria has said things such as 'I can't trust him' and 'He's not going to touch my dog again!'

To me, Gloria looks very distressed, angry and frankly, quite disgusted and disturbed by Michael's behaviour towards Jasper.

In our conversation I paraphase what she has said verbally and then, tentatively, comment on what I think she has communicated non-verbally.

Stage One: defence

- 'No, I'm not upset. I just need you to stop him hurting Jasper!'
- 'Oh no, I never feel angry at him! Maybe irritated but definitely not angry.'
- 'Disgust? I'm not disgusted with him! He's been hurting my dog for God's sake!'

It seems to me at this stage that Gloria is taking my attempts to understand how she feels as criticism of her rather than as a very understandable reaction to Michael's behaviour.

I try to explain my view that her feelings are completely understandable and that I'd feel very negatively about Michael too if someone was hurting a pet of mine.

Stage Two: scepticism/suspicion

Gloria looks at me, confused, as if maybe I am trying to trick her. 'It is a pretty disgusting thing to do isn't it?' 'Don't worry, he doesn't know how angry I am.' 'Ha, you mustn't tell his social worker I said that.'

Gloria appears to be defending herself against the possibility that I might criticise her for having negative feelings towards Michael but is starting to acknowledge that she does have them.

I look at Gloria and show genuine concern. I tell her my thoughts that it must be terrible for her to have a child, that she doesn't know very well, in her home, hurting Jasper, who she has looked after since he was a puppy and has been her faithful friend.

I tell her verbally and non-verbally that having such negative feelings is entirely unsurprising to me. I ask her what the alternative would be. 'What type of person would you be if you knew that was happening and you didn't feel disgusted, angry and upset?'

Stage Three: relief

Gloria looks far more relaxed and she says, 'I do feel like Michael did a really horrible thing and I just want it to stop. He is a loving boy most of the time.'

Gloria seems to feel that her emotions have been understood and she isn't privately condemning, or needing to defend herself, any more. The comments she made about wanting the behaviour to stop and remembering another side to Michael tells me that Gloria has regained some of her empathy for him. We then move on to thinking about the reasons why Michael may have hurt Jasper as he did and what we can do about it.

People in westernised cultures typically find it very difficult to acknowledge their own emotions but they are particularly terrible at acknowledging negative emotions. This is due to a long history of cultures that implicitly use reward-punishment thinking to attempt to discipline the expression of negative emotions. Of course what this process actually does, rather than stopping the emotional response, is to discipline people out of *acknowledging* their negative emotions. The anecdote below demonstrates an everyday example of how people are trained, from an early age, not to express negative emotions.

I was talking with a friend about his five-year-old daughter. She had come home from school with a sticker on her jumper. The sticker had a big yellow, smiley face giving a thumbs-up gesture and the words 'Well Done!' underneath the face. When my friend asked his daughter what she had got the sticker for, she proudly explained that she had fallen over and cut her knee in the playground. She continued by saying that her teacher, in a very kindly way, had praised and congratulated her for her stoic and steadfast refusal to 'make a fuss'. The little girl beamed at her father and said, 'I didn't even cry a little bit, Daddy!'

The result of having legitimate negative emotions that are systematically unacknowledged, and only covertly, non-verbally expressed, is that they are driven underground and emerge in another context when they suddenly appear quite irrational and disproportionate. How many of us haven't, at one time or another, blown up at our partner or one of our children for something minor when we've been stewing about something else that for one reason or another we've not been able truly to acknowledge?

I hope that, by now, it is clear why it is important to take the value judgement out of conversations about emotions. It is important that, when a lack of empathy is evident in carers, it is treated with compassion for them as well as for their children. Damaged empathy is so difficult to acknowledge, even to ourselves, and yet it is so important that carers need to be constantly vigilant for signs of problems with it (Box 2.11).

Box 2.11 Signs of waning empathy

- Feelings of blame and condemnation towards the child.
- Feelings of anger and/or frustration at the child for the problem.
- A desire to lecture, nag and/or scold the child.
- A sense of hopelessness or failure.
- Talking about the child as the problem (as opposed to the problem being the problem, e.g. aggression).
- A strong desire to get the child's behaviour diagnosed in some way.
- Feeling that someone else needs to 'fix' the child, i.e. the carers removing themselves from being part of the solution.
- Loss of curiosity about the problem and the child's experience that led to the problem.

What are the consequences of waning empathy?

There is often a strong pull, when a child's behaviour is stressful, to react rather than respond, that is, it is very tempting for carers to act based on, very understandable, emotional responses, rather than what they know, upon reflection, will enable a child to feel and therefore behave differently in the long term.

Reacting based on reward-punishment thinking can lead to punishing the child because, in subtle ways, it makes the adult feel better. It can also lead to rewarding and praising the child in order to shape their behaviour. Both of these options require carers to evaluate the child rather than focus upon building and strengthening the carer-child relationship.

When carers are distracted by this type of thinking from focusing upon relationship building and do not acknowledge their emotions then it is common for them to get into the mind-set that 'if only I punish hard enough for long enough' the child will do what they want them to. It doesn't take too much imagination to see that this type of thinking, coupled with unspoken resentments and a lack of empathy caused by emotional exhaustion, will only result in damage to the carer-child relationship and potentially worse.

One of the families that I worked with talked in great detail about how different people approached their adopted son's difficulties. Joshua had worked out a wonderfully effective strategy for keeping control of his world by consistently refusing to participate in anything that he was instructed to do. Joshua's adopted parents had managed to stay wonderfully calm and empathic about his difficulties. They understood that his refusals to join in with family life existed for a good reason, even if the family didn't know quite what the reason was or what they could do about it. Joshua's previous head teacher, however, had been drawn into quite a different approach to Joshua and his difficulties. She had spoken with his parents about his 'stubbornness' and how it impacted negatively on his learning and interactions at school and, quite frankly, infuriated everyone around him. This teacher was clearly frustrated and convinced the parents that they needed to work together using reward-punishment thinking to force Joshua out of his strategy; her parting words enthusiastically reassured them, 'Don't worry, we'll break him!'

These reward-punishment strategies rarely work for developmentally traumatised children or for the people who look after them. Even more alarming is the fact that it is this dynamic, which has originated from the child's traumatised ways of 'doing relationships', that sometimes leads otherwise very loving, compassionate carers and professionals into inadvertently replicating the abuse and/or neglect that traumatised the child in the first place (see the relationship replication diagrams throughout the book, e.g. Box 1.4 in Chapter 1).

'I don't recognise myself'/'I've turned into my mother!'

Everybody has patterns of relating to the world that have developed from our early experience; these will inevitably include some idiosyncrasies and emotional 'hang-ups'. If anybody was in doubt of the fact that they had a few of these 'emotional snags' then the perfect way to discover them is to look after a child, particularly a developmentally traumatised child.

Usually these 'emotional snags' don't impede our lives in any way; they are just the bits and pieces of our preferences, sensitivities and tendencies that collect together to form our character. They make us the variously meticulous, sensitive, energetic, witty, impatient, selfless and/ or infuriating people that we are.

This does not mean to suggest that carers are full of hang-ups that cause problems for their children. It does mean, however, that interacting with traumatised children can often trigger the awakening of carers' own emotional snags as well as those of their children. There can, therefore, be different degrees of fit between a child and the person who looks after them. Sometimes an adult's emotional snags can help with those of their child. However, often, because such snags are difficult to understand and acknowledge, they are the elements that make looking after traumatised children more difficult and can lead carers into unhelpful and unempathic ways of approaching their child's difficulties. Box 2.12 may be useful to apply to any of the difficulties that developmentally traumatised children might display in order to explore the feelings and/or emotional snags it brings out in their carers.

Box 2.12 Carers' reactions to problem behaviours

You can either write below or photocopy this page and use it whenever you think that you need to explore your own reactions to your child's difficulty.

What is the problem?

Think of the most recent occasion on which the problem occurred. Think in depth about what was going on, visualise it and spend some time getting into the mood of the occasion. After you've done this for a while then answer the questions below and write your answers down to help you remember when you don't have the time to relive the occasion.

What was going on in your body? *(Did you notice any difference in the sensations in your body? Whereabouts were those sensations? What was your heart doing? Did you feel particularly hot or cold?)*

What were your emotional reactions? *(e.g. angry, overwhelmed, embarrassed, affectionate, excited)*

What did it make you think about? *(e.g. 'I don't know what to do,' 'Why does she do that?', 'He hates me')*

What did it make you want to do? *(e.g. walk away, cuddle the child, shout, tell the child off, etc.)*

Do these reactions feel familiar? *(Are they quite common for you?)*

Did you ever have these reactions in childhood? *(Does this emotional exchange remind you of any of your earlier relationships?)*

Use your responses to help you to be aware of whether your reaction is contributed to by any of your own 'emotional snags' from your past and what your likely responses will be to the behaviour in the future, and to generate new ways of dealing with the difficult behaviour of your child.

I hope that this chapter has helped to explain why empathy is fundamental in enabling carers to move on from reward-punishment thinking and towards a way of relating to developmentally traumatised children that enables them more effectively to manage their children's emotions and therefore their behaviour.

In the following chapters issues will be explored, and exercises and strategies suggested, that will challenge carers' lapses in empathy and elicit sometimes negative emotional reactions. It is useful for carers to notice when they feel themselves wanting to react impulsively to the exercises or to their children and to use the resources, that have been discussed earlier in this chapter, when this happens. This will help carers to think carefully about the empathy in the relationship with their child before they attempt to deal with any challenging behaviours. This will give them the space to respond using the new empathic behaviour management logic rather than react based on reward-punishment thinking.

Box 2.13 Things to remember about maintaining empathy

- Without empathy carers cannot manage the emotions of their traumatised child, nor, therefore, their behaviour.
- Carers should take time to understand why empathy for children traumatised by abuse and neglect can be so hard.
- In a calm period it is useful for carers to work out what their expectations are about relationships and think about how they might compliment or clash with those of their traumatised child.
- It is very important that carers fight to get a good history of their child's experience, keep good notes about it and refresh their memories often.
- Try hard to work out how a child's history makes sense of their current behaviour.
- Carers should be honest with themselves about their feelings about their child and their behaviour.
- Carers' negative feelings towards their child shouldn't be judged. It is important to acknowledge the feelings, and work towards understanding them and developing empathy.
- It is useful for carers to observe and reflect upon their 'emotional snags', which will have developed from their own experience of being parented, and how such snags impact on their emotional reactions towards their child and their empathy for them.
- The first instincts about how to deal with a child's difficult behaviour might be based on, entirely understandable, attempts to stop feeling empathic or to accept a child's invitation to replicate their past experience.
- It is important for carers to work on *responding* to their child's behaviour, in order to enable the child to move away from it, rather than *reacting* to it based on their emotional instincts.
- An informed support network is crucial for carers. It should be invested in for the benefit of carers and their children. It is very useful to identify an 'empathic buddy'.
- Carers should be vigilant for signs of damaged empathy in themselves.

CHAPTER 3

Attention-Seeking Versus Attachment-Seeking

'Ignore him, he's just attention-seeking'

This is a phrase that I hear used very often about the challenging behaviour of children with whom I work. I'm sure carers hear it too; they're quite likely to have said it themselves at one time or another; it makes perfect sense when using reward-punishment thinking. When confronted with a behaviour that should be discouraged, it is a common parenting strategy to ignore it or apply a 'consequence'.

'Attention-seeking' is a term usually applied when a child is persistently trying to be the focus of attention regardless of whether the adult is willing and/or able to give the child that attention. Attention-seeking can take many forms, from a child who talks loudly when their carer is trying to talk to someone else, to one who tells extraordinarily fantastical tales.

Applying the label of attention-seeking to the behaviour of a child who hasn't been afforded sufficient attention in their early years is problematic. Using the language of attention-seeking about a child encourages reward-punishment thinking and discourages curiosity and empathy (and vice versa). If it is concluded that a behaviour is the result of attention-seeking and reward-punishment thinking is applied then it is tantamount to training children to ignore an evolutionarily developed, and essential, survival strategy. Battles between carers and their children about attention are not just conflicts between two people but in fact battles between carers and hundreds of thousands of years of human development; it's really no wonder that it's hard work.

Attention-seeking in a child who has experienced developmental trauma is a very different beast to the attention-seeking of a child who has had positive early experiences of relationships. In children traumatised by abuse and neglect the early drive for closeness has never been sated, so such children often do not move past this developmental stage and into the era of burgeoning independence that is the tumultuous toddler years. Normally developing babies and toddlers are the most driven attention addicts on the planet; they need very close proximity and the immediate assistance of their primary carer at all times. It's no wonder that when such an essential resource is consistently withheld that infants take these unsatisfied needs with them into middle and later childhood.

As a result, when dealing with children who are likely to have missed out on the crucial, intensive doses of attention needed in infancy, it is much more sanity-preserving, useful and, indeed, accurate to reframe children's seemingly relentless desire for attention, as, instead, a desperate need for attachment. They are, in fact, *attachment-seeking*.

Why do babies seek attachment?

Think of the differences between human babies and other mammalian babies. Most mammals develop the ability to seek out food and escape from predators relatively soon after birth. Human infants lack these crucial survival skills, so they need to have others. As human babies can't meet their own needs, their ability to survive depends upon their ability to stay close enough to an adult who can.

Therefore, the primary preoccupation, for human infants, is their ability to persuade the adults around them to keep them close by any means necessary. The need for physical closeness is as primal and crucial for babies as the need for food and safety because closeness ensures those things. In babyhood the ability to keep adults close is the only way to exert the control over them that is necessary for the baby's survival. This is, fundamentally, why humans are such social animals and why relationships can be our greatest source of pleasure and comfort but can also be the cause of upset and, occasionally, our most crippling pain.

What is attachment-seeking?

Babies have many ways of ensuring that they get attention from, and closeness to, their primary carer. Before reading ahead too far stop and think about the things that babies do to get attention from their carers (Box 3.1).

Box 3.1 Examples of 'attachment-seeking behaviours' in developmentally traumatised children

- Competing with siblings.
  - Children have often had past experience of needing to compete for limited amount of crucial attention; this strategy is invariably applied by these children in their new homes.
- Fighting.
- Spitefulness.
- Telling tales.
- False allegations.
- Looking for, or creating, confrontation.
  - This may lead to behaviours such as lying, stealing, etc. All of these provocative behaviours are very difficult for carers to ignore so they are very successful in achieving proximity when it is needed.
- Persistent desire to help.
  - This is a type of attachment-seeking that is quite attractive and endearing to carers and so it is likely to be successful in getting attention.
- Incessant/nonsensical questioning.
  - Carers often think that children who repeatedly ask them the same question, or ask questions that don't make sense, are doing so because of memory problems or some kind of cognitive deficit. Often it's a simple, effective way of encouraging interaction or starting a conversation with their carer.

All of these attachment-seeking behaviours can also fulfil other psychological functions for developmentally traumatised children but, almost always, they are strategies, unconsciously designed, to bring their carer, or someone else, close to them.

I'm sure most people can recall an occasion on which they've been at the supermarket, sat in a doctors' waiting room or in some other public place and seen an alert baby. Babies have an incredible power to captivate everyone around them with their intense eye-contact. I remember a recent occasion, when I was at a primary school assembly, to which a parent had brought her baby. The baby boy was propped against his mother's chest peering backwards over her shoulder. He had beautiful, piercing eyes and was staring intently at me as I gave him big smiles with wide eyes and exaggerated facial expressions. It was only after some time that I paused to notice that I was joined in this daft and compulsive behaviour by four other adults, in the immediate vicinity, all of whom were making equally big-eyed, expressive cartoon faces at the little boy who simply stared, mesmerised, back at us all.

Another very powerful, unconscious, attachment-seeking strategy that babies use to bring their carers close is crying. Try the exercise in Box 3.2 to really get to grips with how powerful a baby's cry can be.

Box 3.2 Baby's cry exercise: Part One

There are two ways of doing this exercise. If you have access to a baby then the live experience of this exercise is far more powerful. If you don't then try conjuring a baby to mind.

Live experience

If you have easy access to a baby then take the opportunity to listen carefully the next time he or she cries. Just a few seconds of hearing a baby cry will do for this exercise so there's no need for them to be left crying for longer than they normally would be.

Conjure the baby to mind

If you are imaging, close your eyes and spend a few minutes visualising the crying baby; this is not a baby that has any particular difficulties or is experiencing any abuse or neglect. Where is the baby? Is it a boy or a girl? What is the baby wearing? What do the baby's eyes and hair look like? Imagine the characteristics of the baby's face, the baby's eyes, nose, mouth, ears, cheeks, etc.

Take time to imagine the sounds and smells that might be around. Now imagine that you are listening to the baby's growing wail, listen to the cry for a few seconds, notice how the cry changes in pitch and volume.

Notice your reaction

When you have either found a baby you can listen to or spent some time carefully picturing your imaginary baby, make a note of your responses to the following:

What does your body do? *(Where can you feel these things in your body? Does the feeling come and go or stay around?)*

What emotions do you experience? *(It's often very hard to separate emotions and thoughts but for this part try hard to stick solely with feeling, e.g. anger, excitement, sadness)*

What are you thinking about as you listen to the baby? *(e.g. 'What do I fancy for dinner?', 'Yesterday was stressful')*

What does the baby's cry make you want to do?

In the light of your responses to this exercise think about the history of your child. Your child's need for attention in their early days, weeks and months was a powerful and urgent one.

No matter what their experience was, your child will have worked very, very hard to have been unignorable and to be looked after well enough; their survival depended on getting it right. Your child would have resorted to responses that would have been as urgent and as desperate as a bear caught in a trap; desperate times would indeed have elicited desperate measures. Either the bear becomes impossible to ignore, takes matters into his own hands and frees himself (and accepts the severe consequences) or he becomes hopeless and gives himself up to whatever might befall him.

The compulsive instincts that most people experience to attend to the eye-contact and smiles of an attentive and alert baby, or to the cries of a baby who is distressed, are evolutionarily programmed. The desperate attempts of traumatised children to get attention from adults are communications of the same need for attachment but, due to adult assumptions about how to parent, that is, in accordance with a child's chronological age, frequently create reactions that do not meet the child's attachment needs.

However, the universal human instincts, developed over hundreds of thousands of years of human evolution, are much more informative about how to react to the distress of a child than the relatively new obsession with supernannies and star charts. Reward-punishment thinking is important, and our children do need a certain amount of training, but their primitive preoccupation to cling on to their caregiver needs to be attended to, and exhausted, before this type of thinking can be usefully added into the parenting toolbox.

Developmentally traumatised children have had to be rescued from their home situation. Even babies that are removed at birth experience the acute distress of separation and suffer the consequences. This means that, despite their urgent and frantic attempts, they failed to get their caregiver(s) to act as they needed them to, that is, in a way that would have allowed the child to relax and not have to work so hard to get their needs met. The child's needs for attention and attachment were not met in these crucial early days, months and years and so they continue to seek them in the only way they know; they then anticipate the responses from the caregiver that they have learned to expect (Box 3.3).

Box 3.3 Baby's cry exercise: Part Two

Having done Part One of this exercise (Box 3.2), you will be better able to understand your child's thoughts and feelings (as separate and distinct from your own). Do not attempt to do this for your child until you have done it for yourself.

Think again about your crying baby and make empathic guesses about:

What was going on in the baby's body? (e.g. red face, tense muscles)

What do you think their emotional reactions were? (the ones they showed outwardly and the ones they didn't)

What do you think your baby was thinking?

What do you think their fears were at this time?

Having understood that the 'attention-seeking' of developmentally traumatised children is more accurately viewed as a *need* for greater levels of proximity and attention, these behaviours will henceforth be labelled attachment-seeking behaviours.

Attachment-seeking and you

Following on from the previous statements it has been established that more attention is better for developmentally traumatised children. It is now necessary to think about how to go about providing children with the attachment experiences that they require. Half of this battle is managing the demands that such needs place upon carers so that they can sustain their provision of attachment experiences. The physical and emotional challenges of dealing with a young baby and the allowances that are made in order to do it were explored in Chapter 2. It's perhaps easier to understand the long-term difficulties of looking after the attachment, attention and stimulation needs of an older developmentally traumatised child, if we try to imagine ourselves doing the same for a baby over an equivalent length of time.

Ironically, the invitation, by reward-punishment thinking, is to give attachment-seeking children less attention as a result of their behaviour rather than the greater amount that they need. Carers are drawn into using strategies that are based on the assumption of 'give them an inch and they'll take a mile'. I hope it is starting to become clear that developmentally traumatised children need, instead, the principle of 'give them a mile so that eventually they'll only need an inch'.

Whilst traumatised children may appear to be bottomless pits of attention, they are not, but often they are very, very deep ones. Consequently the task of carers of these children is to set about filling the deep hole left by their past experiences. The key is to accept, from the beginning, that this cannot be done quickly. Most carers are desperate to make a positive difference to their children as quickly as possible; an entirely understandable and laudable aim. However, progress in this area will take time and so piling all of your hopes into the immediate future can only lead to being disheartened.

Reward-punishment responses to attachment-seeking

The way in which parents and carers are typically told to deal with 'attention-seeking behaviour' is to respond to it as though the cause of the behaviour is unimportant, that is, that, regardless of what caused it, a certain way of responding to it will stop the behaviour. Reward-punishment thinking leads carers to believe that the praise and/or reward of desired behaviours will cause an increase in the behaviour whilst punishment of it will cause a decrease.

There are many concerns currently being raised about the appropriateness of such methods for all children in light of recent neuroscientific discoveries. However, this 'black box' approach to children's minds fails spectacularly when applied to the minds of developmentally traumatised children. Their minds, and therefore their needs, are different to those of other children due to the disruption to their development.

So, what happens if reward-punishment thinking is used with children traumatised by abuse and/or neglect? Many carers report that attempts to ignore 'attention-seeking' in fostered and adopted children actually seems to escalate the problem. This is because, in ignoring a child's attachment-seeking, carers are inadvertently replicating the parenting behaviour that caused the attachment-seeking, that is, the child's need, in infancy, to seek close proximity to their parent was not prioritised and so has increased the child's need to seek out proximity to their attachment figure (Box 3.4).

Box 3.4 Relationship replication – attachment-seeking
Birth family experiences

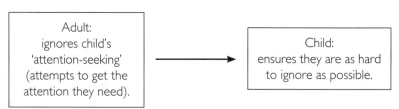

The birth parent rarely interacts with the child. The child develops a strategy of active attachment-seeking (e.g. crying, being difficult to settle, staying very close, making themselves very useful, wanting constant contact with their parent, shouting, aggression), which cannot be ignored.

Foster/Adoptive family experience

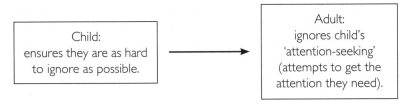

The child uses the strategy of demanding attention via active attachment-seeking. The carer feels controlled so distances themselves from the child and/or carer follows reward-punishment thinking and uses the 'ignoring bad behaviour' technique.

SUMMARY: The neglectful/inattentive parenting has led the child to seek attachment/proximity. The child has unconsciously invited the carer to ignore them. The carer has accepted the invitation.

If the traumatised child does not adopt the attachment-seeking strategy and is successfully trained not to seek constant, close proximity to another person, then that child would have serious difficulty in keeping themselves safe, understanding and engaging with other people. Some children do take this route (i.e. they are avoidantly attached) and so, quite the opposite of the attachment-seeking child, they need to be supported in developing the inclination to look to their carer for nurture and protection.

So, instead of ignoring what is in a child's mind their attachment-seeking behaviour can be used as a window into their emotional world.

Therefore, in the case of developmentally traumatised children, 'Ignore him, he's just attention-seeking' just doesn't make any sense. Effectively, this statement means 'Ignore him, he's trying to survive.' The exclamations that make sense of the attachment-seeking behaviour of developmentally traumatised children, are, more accurately, 'Thank goodness you're still trying to get looked after' and 'I'm so relieved that you're still trying to survive.'

I often hear concerns that children will, in some way, become addicted to all the attention that I encourage carers to give and then suffer when they get out into the 'real' world, where they won't get that level of attention any more. Remember though, that parenting this kind of trauma is a therapeutically developmental process; children can only stand a chance of moving beyond the need for constant attention when they have been afforded the chance of all of the attention that a newborn baby needs. The positive, psychological and neurological, effects of the ample attention given in infancy are much slower when they are replicated in older, developmentally traumatised, children but they can be achieved.

There really is no benefit to a child traumatised by abuse and/or neglect of trying to wean them off attention. Just like all children, they will make it all too clear when they've had enough of your company by seeking it less and less. There are very few 17-year-olds (who have had enough care and attention in early life) who still want to sit on their mother's knee while watching TV and it is not because anybody has disciplined them into not doing it.

Therefore, attachment-seeking makes sense for many developmentally traumatised children and it is not a behaviour we should try to rid them of using reward-punishment thinking. Consequently, the very sensible and laudable concerns that carers have for their children, that is, that they will be doing a bad job by giving their children 'too much' attention and/or they will not be equipping their children with the social skills they need in order for them not to be 'an attention seeker', have now disappeared. In effect, carers don't have to worry about that aspect of parenting any more because the more attention they give their child the better it is for them. However, this does not mean that it is an easy task.

It is also worthwhile briefly considering the consequences of not providing the attention/attachment experiences that developmentally traumatised children crave. If such a child is working as hard as they can to get those attachment experiences from their carer and they are not successful, the strategy will need to be adapted. This will mean either finding new ways to get the carer to give the child the attention that they need or finding it elsewhere. A child's unmet need to attachment-seek can lead to many other problematic behaviours (see Box 3.5).

Box 3.5 Potential consequences of not responding empathically to 'attention-seeking'

- Peer relationship problems.
- Apparent lack of social skills.
- Low self-esteem.
- Sexual vulnerability/exploitation.

- Early pregnancy.
- Gang membership.
- Overeating.
- Drug misuse.
- Alcohol misuse.
- Vulnerability to domestic violence.

Most carers understand that their children need more attention than other children do. Many will try very hard to give their child enough attention but often it becomes too draining to sustain and the carer starts to feel crushed under the weight of the child's need and their own feelings of frustration, hopelessness and/or irritation. As a result, a more structured approach can be enormously useful. It may also necessitate an adjustment of your expectations. It may be that your child will always need more attention than some but everybody is on that continuum somewhere.

Having an understanding of why a child is attachment-seeking often leads carers into developing new, very different ways of behaving with their children. It is much easier to have empathy for a child displaying a challenging behavioural trait once its cause is understood and its legitimacy has become clear. However, as I have discussed in the sections above, this understanding and acceptance only goes some of the way towards making the change. There also has to be an acceptance that using strategies that give children the attention and attachment experiences they need and demand is thoroughly exhausting. Having said this, many carers tell me that adopting reward-punishment techniques is not only extremely exhausting but also frustrating and often infuriating to the point that it is damaging to their relationship with their child.

Empathic behaviour management strategies
How to deal with attachment-seeking
Figure 3.1 demonstrates there are several factors that help us to understand attachment-seeking in traumatised children; the most influential are in bold, though the other factors may be influential to lesser extents.

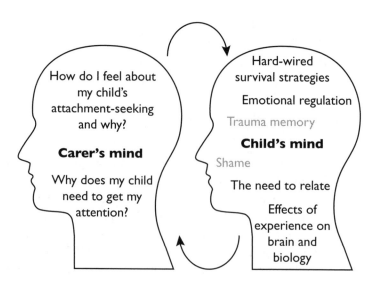

Figure 3.1 EBM model of attachment-seeking

The following section on strategies is by no means exhaustive. It is my hope that, using the EBM model, the previous chapters and the first half of this chapter, you will be able to develop your own creative solutions to help you and your child with their attachment-seeking.

EBM for carers

All of the following are preventative strategies that can be used to help carers to prepare themselves to deal with their own reactions to attachment-seeking.

PREVENTATIVE STRATEGIES FOR CARERS

How does your child's attachment-seeking make you feel and why?

The first challenge for carers is to focus on developing their understanding of their own reactions to their child's attachment-seeking. Using Boxes 2.11 (in Chapter 2) and 3.2 may help carers to understand how their child's behaviour, and their own reactions to it, make sense and will help to increase their empathy when it's waning.

WHY DOES MY CHILD NEED TO GET MY ATTENTION?
HOW DOES THEIR BEHAVIOUR MAKE SENSE?

The second task for carers, before they start applying their ideas to their child, is to try to work out how the child's behaviour makes sense. What must they have experienced, what preconceptions must they have had about their carers and the world for their behaviour to be a sensible, adaptive strategy? It is likely that the answer to this will lie in one or several of the influences highlighted in the 'Child's mind' section of the EBM model (Box 3.6).

In the case of attachment-seeking it is very important to manage your child's behaviour empathically. A crucial part of that is to manage your own emotional reaction to the attachment-seeking so that the empathy doesn't run out. This is of particular importance at times when you have identified that your empathy is waning.

The new bucket

This is a metaphor that offers a way of viewing children who demand a great deal of attention from their carers.

Box 3.6 The new bucket

It is useful to see trying to meet the attention needs of a developmentally traumatised child as being like trying to fill a bucket.

It's a bucket that needs filling and when you get hold of it it's completely empty; as a result it's going to take quite some time to fill up. You set about filling it with water from your own bucket. To keep doing this you have to make sure your bucket gets filled up regularly from somewhere. However, you reassure yourself that you can cope with an empty bucket for a while, just while you get this other one filled up. You rationalise that the new bucket is in greater need than yours after all.

It's only after quite some time, of dutifully filling the new bucket, that you notice that not only is the new bucket still virtually empty, but that your own bucket is also empty. When you think about it you realise that the new bucket fills up sometimes but then the water slowly disappears. 'Well, what's the point in bothering?! I'm trying so hard and it's not working!' At this point you consider that the most sensible option would be to stop trying to put water in the new bucket; indeed, maybe it will be fine without water...?

Another possibility is that the bucket has a tiny leak. If this were the case then maybe there is a way of filling the new bucket and making sure that our bucket stays full too. However, you need something thicker, more substantial than water, something that will not leak out as easily. How about jam? The jam will still leak out but much more slowly and eventually, given enough time, the seeds will collect together and the sugar will crystallise and form a seal over the tiny hole in the new bucket. If that happens it's much more likely that the bucket will be able to hold water without your help. In addition, to make sure your bucket doesn't get drained dry you also need to make time to fill the new bucket regularly, but with small amounts at a time rather than constantly trying to fill it to the top.

The jam is definitely more effective then water at filling the new bucket but it is harder to get hold of and it takes more time, thought and inconvenience to make sure we have enough. However, if we definitely want to fill the bucket, using jam is probably the most effective solution.

This metaphor can be a useful way of understanding how to more successfully meet the needs of your attachment-seeking child. Rather than giving your child the attention that you would typically give to children (the water) the new bucket helps us to see that you will need to make a more concerted effort and work harder to give your child more substantial doses of attention (the jam). All of this whilst remaining mindful of the effort that you are putting in, the toll it takes on you and, if you're not careful, the relationship with your child.

EBM for children

The following strategies address children's dual needs, for responsive, flexible access to their attachment figure and regular, predictable attention (see Box 3.7). Working on both of these elements, that is, using strategies from the responsive and preventative EBM sections (below), is the most powerful route to enabling your child to become more independent of you.

Box 3.7 Your child's drives to seek closeness to you

Think of the most recent occasion that your child was attention/attachment-seeking and answer the following questions in relation to that occasion.

What do you think that your child was feeling at the time that the attachment-seeking started?

i.e. 'What must my child be feeling to make behaving this way make sense?'

Try very hard to set aside your own thoughts and feelings about the behaviour and tune into your child's internal world. In doing this you may have to fight the urge to write down the emotions that, superficially, appear to be the most logical thing for your child to be feeling.

> What do you think were your child's biggest concerns at the time of the attachment-seeking?

> *i.e. 'What must my child be worried about to make behaving in this way make sense?'*

Again, suspend your own feelings and tune into what part of their abusive past makes sense of their behaviour.

> How could attachment-seeking behaviour make good sense as a response to your child's feelings and concerns?

Carers may find, when implementing these strategies, that their child starts to attachment-seek more, before they can start to cope with less proximity. This may be due to the child's excitement about the novelty or it may be that the child has been able to awaken a belief that what they need is really out there and so wants to gorge themselves before it is all taken away again. Often with approaches which seek to understand a child's inner world the presenting problem can get worse before it gets better but using these structured approaches should help you to cope.

RESPONSIVE EBM FOR CHILDREN

Give as much attention as you can

The first point to make about dealing with a child who seeks attention is to give as much as you possibly can without allowing it to become self-defeating, that is, it is important that carers don't become so exhausted, frustrated, resentful, etc. that they lose their empathy and undermine their previous good work. The substance of that attention could be anything that brings child and carer closer together, ideally something with which both can have fun; smiling together and sharing joy is hugely powerful. Physical contact can also be enormously beneficial in creating positive experiences for children, so the odd touch on the shoulder or hair ruffle can be useful but, what is even better, when they feel right for child and carer, are hugs and hand holding.

Intimacy: attentive nurture strategies

Often children traumatised by abuse and/or neglect seek attention when they are expected to do age-appropriate self-care tasks, e.g. teeth-cleaning, bathing. If this is the case then it may be an indication that the child is attempting, unconsciously, to communicate that they need intimate nurture from their carer, as would instinctively be given to a much younger child. Box 3.8 contains examples of intimate attention that may help in such cases.

Box 3.8 Examples of attentive nurture strategies

- Cuddles.
- Cleaning a child's teeth for them.
- Washing them in the bath.
- Brushing their hair (gently).
- Putting talcum powder or moisturiser on your child.
- Feeding your child, whilst they sit on your knee (much as you would a baby).
- Holding and rocking your child.
- Singing nursery rhymes.

In situations in which *attentive nurture* strategies may be useful, it is advisable for foster carers to consult with their respective agencies to discuss their Safe-Care Policy. It is important, however, that if carers identify that their child's attachment-seeking is linked with occasions of self-care then carers should help agencies to understand why using such strategies is important.

Carers should pay close attention to their child's attachment-seeking behaviour and the child's responses to these strategies. Even if the child's behaviour indicates that these strategies would be useful and the child's hypothetical responses appear positive, carers should remain attentive to how their child responds when they try to implement the strategies. It is important to remain mindful that traumatised children may have very different, conscious and unconscious, ideas of what intimacy and nurture means.

Using these strategies can feel a little odd for carers when they are used with an older child but it is useful to try them and see how children respond; it is often very surprising how naturally children take to nurturing strategies.

Empathic commentary

The 'EBM for carers' section, above, is likely to have helped carers to understand why their child is seeking attachment experiences with them. This understanding can be used by carers to convey to their children, first, that they understand their child's behaviour and feelings, and second, what their understandings of the behaviour and feelings are. This will be valuable to a traumatised child because they are unlikely to understand, for themselves, the reasons why they behave as they do. This, in a nutshell, is *empathic commentary*.

I will talk about empathic commentary in other chapters. Whenever it is used it is very important to follow the golden rules (Box 3.9).

Box 3.9 Empathic commentary: golden rules

- Work hard to be empathic. Despite what the child's behaviour might make carers feel, it is important to concentrate on the child's emotions and how their experience makes sense of the emotions and behaviours.

- It is important for carers to try to mirror their child's facial expression and the emotion that makes sense of their behaviour, if these are different, and the child's energy levels, in a calm, contained way.

- Carers should endeavour to demonstrate their empathy with words but, more importantly, with their tone of voice and body language.

- It is useful for carers to be tentative about how they convey their understanding of the child's emotions and behaviour.

- Be brief and don't overcomplicate what is said in the commentary.

- There is no need for carers to ask their child questions; if what the carer says is tentative then their child will have an opportunity to correct them.

- If the emotion is ambiguous or contradictory then carers should commentate on this ambiguity rather than trying to force one single interpretation of the child's emotional state.

- Avoid using comments that either praise or chastise. Try to be judgement-neutral.

- *Responsive empathic commentary*, i.e. commentary for use *during* the child's difficulty, should be brief, clear and concise.

- *Preventative empathic commentary*, i.e. commentary for non-problematic times, can be slightly wordier and contain more explanation. It should still only be one or two sentences.

Using empathic commentary with attachment-seeking children will help them to understand why they need to be close to you, in general and at specific times of stress. It will enable children to accept their own need to be near to their carers and, over time, help them to move beyond it, towards greater independence. Box 3.10 provides some examples of empathic commentary that carers can use with their attachment-seeking child.

Box 3.10 Responsive empathic commentary for attachment-seeking

The following are examples of empathic commentary statements that can be useful in managing the attachment-seeking of traumatised children. Use them to come up with statements that work for you and your child.

- 'Oh gosh, it makes you feel so worried when I can't be here chatting to you. I'm so sorry.'
- 'You've been on your own so much that it feels like you need to be close to me all of the time. I'm so sorry that I can't be with you all the time.'
- 'You're really struggling to get your teeth cleaned aren't you? You've always had to look after yourself without much grown-up help. I wonder if it would feel nice if I helped you with it.'
- 'You're shouting at me lots! You've always had to work very hard to get grown-ups to pay attention to you haven't you? OK, let's go and do something fun together.'
- 'Wow! You're really angry with me because I'm talking on the phone! I'm sorry that you can't have all of my attention all of the time. That's horrible for you; it really doesn't feel fair does it?'

Attachment surrogacy

On those occasions when carers simply cannot give their child the attention that they crave, and after using empathic commentary to help the child understand their own behaviour, carers might like to try an *attachment surrogate*.

An attachment surrogate can take a range of forms but it is, in essence, an object that bridges the gap between carer and child when they have to be apart. This could be a cuddly toy that the child can take with them. This toy should be integrated as an ordinary part of the relationship between carer and child, for example, a teddy bear that carer and child both cuddle and look after at different times.

Another method of attachment surrogacy is for carers to give their child an object that they know is genuinely important to the carer in some way. This will convey to the child that, even though their carer is not able to be with them or giving them attention at that time, they know that they will definitely see their carer again because they will need to get the important object back or at least know that it is safe.

Sometimes developmentally traumatised children find a sensory reminder of their carer to be a useful way of overcoming their need for immediate attention. For example, at night it may be a comfort for children to sleep with something that smells of their carer, perhaps the t-shirt the carer wore during the day. Other examples are a picture of the child and carer together or a voice recording of the carer reading a story or giving the child a message. Anything that bridges the gap between carer and child and taps into one of the child's senses can be a sensory attachment surrogate.

The Limpet Game

The Limpet Game is an opportunity for carers and their children to have fun together when the child is attachment-seeking. Carers can use this as a responsive or a preventative strategy to deal with attachment-seeking. If the Limpet Game is used as a responsive strategy, then carers should first use empathic commentary to convey to their child that they understand that the child's behaviour is a result of their need to be close to their carer and what the carer believes to be the cause.

The objective of the Limpet Game is for carer and child to stay in close physical contact for ten minutes. If the child is young enough they could stand on the front of their carer's feet and cling on to their legs. Half of the fun will be working out how carer and child can get the closest they can, like a limpet would! Carer and child have to stick together for the full ten minutes; both people are on the same team and both have to work hard at it. It might be tempting to treat it like a competition but it's very important that you work together, so it is important that there is no teasing or attempts to escape.

When carers set up the rules with their child they should get excited and show enthusiasm to get the child on board with the game. Then carer and child can set a timer together that makes a noise. Both should then decide together on the task they have to complete whilst they are stuck together; this can be anything that comes to mind, even practical tasks, for example, hanging out washing or doing the washing up; any task, as long as it wouldn't be dangerous.

When the ten minutes has passed, the Limpet Game is over but carer and child can carry on spending time together doing the washing up, or whatever the task was, but without the need for constant physical contact.

The Limpet Game can also be played with carers and two children if they are both craving attention at the same time.

PREVENTATIVE EBM FOR CHILDREN

Pre-empting your child's need for attention

Often children's need to seek closeness with their carer can be pre-empted. Indeed, identifying it before their need for attention escalates beyond that which carers can cope with is very important. So, if carers can read the signs it will be advantageous to give their child some concentrated attention before their behaviour becomes problematic. You can use any of the strategies suggested in this chapter or other creative solutions that you come up with in response to reading and understanding the theory behind children's attention-seeking behaviour.

Attachment time menu

For developmentally traumatised children who crave their carer's attention the *attachment time menu* is a strategy to use in order to prevent your child's attachment-seeking behaviour.

Attachment time is a short period of time, scheduled into the week, for carers and their children to spend time together. Carers should start by working out when they can have this one-to-one time with their child on a regular basis. I suggest, for children who are old enough and have the attention to cope with it, beginning with once a day, every day for an hour. For younger children, and those who struggle to sustain attention, 20 minutes upwards would be better (but try to stick with a consistent length of time).

Attachment time should be at a predictable time of day when carers know that they can devote time to their child completely. Carers who have more than one child may need to find a time when someone else can look after the other child or at least when you can be sure that they will be able to occupy themselves. Interruptions and distractions should be prevented as much as possible, e.g. telephones should be unplugged and/or turned off as it is important that carers are able completely to devote their attention to their child. Attachment time should take place away from the rest of the family and in a room that does not have any electrical gadgets that could be distracting, e.g. TVs, computers, etc.

When carers have identified which time of day and in which room the attachment time sessions can take place then carer and child can start to work out what activities they will have on their menu. It is useful for carers to sit down with their child and come up with a range of activities that will fill the allocated time. These activities can be anything that is shared (see Box 3.11 for examples) but homework should not be included. Homework is something that requires adults to be directive with their children and is not necessarily something children will consistently enjoy. Attachment time should be a time for fun and should be led by the child. Carers can share with their child and negotiate, if necessary, about where and when attachment time will be and then the details should be written down somewhere very obvious to solidify the child's understanding of the regularity and predictability of attachment time, for example, by making a note on a calendar or in the child's diary or by writing a big note and sticking it to the fridge.

Box 3.11 Examples of activities for an attachment time menu

- Playing with building blocks.
- Puzzles.
- Imaginary games with character toys.
- Ball games.
- Trampolining games.
- Face painting.
- Make-overs and hair-styling.
- Board games.
- Playing musical instruments.
- Telling stories to one another.
- Computer games that are genuinely reciprocal, i.e. that encourage carer and child to interact with one another.

Consistency is very important when using attachment time. Any slips may lead children to question the dependability of this activity with their carer and so will escalate the child's attachment-seeking and impact negatively on the carer-child relationship. Attachment time can be portable; it only needs the carer, the child and the activities from the menu that have been agreed upon and a quiet room. If there are any changes that are unavoidable, though these should be rare, carers should prepare their child thoroughly for the change and use empathic commentary to help the child to deal with the upset it may cause.

To build up the attachment time menu carers should think with their child about all the activities that the child might enjoy doing with their carer, and write each of them down on a card; the child might like to draw pictures of the activities on the cards. Anything that helps the child to feel ownership of attachment time is a good thing. It would be useful to have at least ten activities to choose from on the attachment time menu. Keep the cards special and safe in a box or a bag.

When it comes to the allocated attachment time, carers should encourage their child to choose a few activities from the attachment time menu for them both to do together that day. However, carers should be the judge of how many activities they think will fill the time that has been agreed.

Carers can help their child to fully enjoy the time and do their best to have as much fun together as possible. Carers can use five and then two-minute warnings to assist their child in understanding that the end of attachment time is approaching. The end of attachment time can be quite stressful and upsetting for children. If it is, then carers can remind their child that they will have attachment time again very soon and demonstrate the point by showing them that the next attachment time is written down. Carers can even start to encourage them to think about what activities they may like to choose for next time.

Carers may find, over time, that their child needs less and less attachment time. As the months go by and their bucket becomes less leaky (see Box 3.6), it may be possible to reduce the amount of attachment times per week. However, it is important that carers are led in their decision-making by the attachment-seeking behaviour of their child. Only when they are seeking attachment much less should carers start to reduce the sessions. Having said that, it is useful to integrate attachment time sessions into everyday life and keep them in your routine, to one extent or another, permanently.

Attachment time: Traffic light system

The *traffic light system* can be a useful addition to attachment time for children who are particularly struggling in terms of their need for attention and proximity to their carer. It is a way of enabling attachment time to be responsive as well as preventative and of helping children to communicate directly with their carer about their attachment needs.

To use the traffic light system, carers will need to give their child small red, amber and green cards that the child can carry with them. Carers may find it useful to have several sets around the house to enable their child to access them quickly, when they need them. The meanings of the cards are detailed in Box 3.12.

Box 3.12 Traffic light system: card definitions

Red   'I need your attention now!'

When this card is produced carers should drop what they are doing and have some devoted contact with their child; they may need a cuddle or some other immediate comfort. Carers can use empathic commentary to try to communicate to their child that they understand that they are feeling needy, and why carers think that they may be.

Carers should give their child as much attention as they can and respond to the child's verbal and non-verbal communication. It may be that the child will feel much better after just a few minutes; however, on some occasions it may take some time.

If, after the carer's immediate response, they are not able to give the child quite as much time as they need, the carer should help the child to understand that they can have more time after the carer has completed the task that they are engaged in at the time and then follow it up. This must not be forgotten!

Amber   'I need your attention when you've finished what you're doing.'

When the amber card is produced, carers should tell the child, as precisely as they can, how long they'll have to wait until the carer can give the child some devoted time. It should be within an hour of the child presenting the card. When the time for the amber response comes carers can follow the guidelines given for the red card (above).

Green   'I'm letting you know that I could do with some devoted attention but I think I can wait until our next session of attachment time.'

When children present green cards carers should be mindful that their child is trying very hard to cope with their feelings without devoted attachment time but that they may need little bits of support. Carers can, for example, encourage their child to join them in what they are doing or encourage someone else to spend some time with the child.

Once carers have helped their child to understand the meanings of the cards and how to use them, the child should be trusted to hand the appropriate card to their carer in order to communicate their attachment needs when they need to.

Many carers are sceptical about this approach as they imagine that their child will only use the red card and constantly want immediate attention. This is sometimes the case, but this exercise of power typically fades quite quickly and is, in fact, an integral part of the development of children's understanding about how responsive to their needs their carer will really be. It is often surprising how effective this technique can be and how honest and sparing children are with the cards. The use of the traffic light cards by the child, paired with the carer's empathic commentary, will help the child to internalise an understanding of their legitimate need for closeness and also provides a tangible marker for how the child's need to attachment-seek is progressing.

The principles of the traffic light cards can also be used with children who do not have the cognitive ability to use the actual cards. Carers can use the traffic light guidelines to assess the levels of attention that their child might need, but, in this case, carers will need to read their child's emotions and behaviour honestly and respond accordingly. It is very difficult, when using this version of the traffic light system, not to give into the temptation to respond based on the level of attention that is easiest for carers to give, rather than make an honest appraisal of what level the child needs. Whilst giving the child control of the cards is, by far, the better option if carers do have to use the latter version, then they should be *very* mindful, and guard against the pitfalls, of determining the level of attention their child needs themselves, rather than responding to their cues.

Box 3.13: Things to remember about attention-seeking versus attachment-seeking

Understanding why it makes sense

- The phrase 'attention-seeking' leads people into reward-punishment thinking and impedes the ability to think empathically.
- Babies need an incredible amount of attention in order to:
  - stay safe from predators
  - ensure they are fed
  - enable their brains to develop as they should
  - develop the ability to recognise and regulate their own emotions
  - develop a positive understanding of themselves
  - develop a positive understanding of relationships.
- Children who have been abused and/or neglected invariably haven't had enough, good-quality attention.
- Children who haven't had enough attention carry on needing it, for all the reasons above, until they have their need sated.
- Attention-seeking, in developmentally traumatised children, is attachment-seeking.
- The phrase 'attachment-seeking' helps people to feel more empathic and drives them to understand why the behaviour occurs.
- Developmentally traumatised children need as many attachment experiences as carers can give them.
- Giving traumatised children a sufficient amount of proximity and attachment experience is very difficult and can lead to carers losing empathy and giving up.

Understanding what to do

- EBM for carers:
  - Preventative strategies:
    - Carers need to have a thorough understanding of how their child's attachment-seeking makes them feel and why.
    - Carers need to work at understanding why their child needs to get their attention and how their behaviour makes sense.
- EBM for children:
  - Responsive strategies:
    - Carers should give their child as much attention as they can whilst remaining mindful of their own limits.

- ○ The levels of intimacy can be increased by using attentive nurture strategies.
- ○ Empathic commentary (this can also be used as a preventative strategy).
- ○ Attachment surrogates.
- ○ The Limpet Game.
- ○ Preventative strategies:
  - ▪ The child's need for attention can be pre-empted by tuning into their communications and body language.
  - ▪ Attachment time menu.
  - ▪ Traffic light system.

CHAPTER 4

The Red Mist

One of the most common issues that I am asked to try to help with is the 'angry outbursts' or 'meltdowns' of children traumatised by abuse and/or neglect. These can be some of the most distressing, frightening and, frankly, disturbing issues in the lives of traumatised children.

There is a complexity to the anger of traumatised children that is very different to the anger seen in other children. The anger is often more extreme, more sudden in its onset and usually very much more difficult for carers to put a stop to, both in the immediate sense and in the longer term. I call this type of behaviour a 'rage outburst'. These are different to anger because they often have a very out-of-control, primal quality to them. I have used the analogy of the red mist in the title of this chapter, as it is a useful way of communicating the separation between children and the world around them when they are in the grip of their rage.

These children can also be described as 'Jekyll and Hyde' children, as they seem to become quickly enraged and often are just as quick to revert to their typical selves. Carers have described to me, in vivid detail, seemingly physiological changes in their children when they are at the mercy of a rage outburst. One carer said, 'It's literally like the colour of his eyes changes' and another described losing recognition for her child, 'The shape of his face seems to change'. These changes, though challenging to believe, let alone understand, do make sense when consideration is given to the profound physiological changes that have to take place in the human body in order for people to protect themselves in the most terrifying of situations. The pupils of their eyes will dilate in order to take in more light and therefore more information about their surroundings and the muscles in the face will tense and flex in atypical ways to create a more fearsome visage.

It is very useful for carers to understand how to deal with rage outbursts effectively and with empathy. However, in some of the more extreme cases, particularly if carers believe their child, themselves or anyone else to be at risk, it is advisable to seek attachment-based therapeutic support for the rage outbursts.

What is the red mist?

There is a great variety in the types of rage outbursts that are seen in developmentally traumatised children. The following examples demonstrate the range of severity and character of the rage outbursts of traumatised children.

Kayla

Kayla was a five-year-old girl living with her single female foster carer, Diane. She came into care when she was two and a half years old, after her parents had been found to be unable to care for her. Kayla's parents had been using a range of illegal drugs and, as a result of that lifestyle, lots of strangers had come in and out of the house. The police attended the young family's home on several occasions after calls about violence at the property. Overall, as a result of all of these things Kayla's parents were largely unavailable to their young daughter.

Kayla's outbursts of rage were most severe when she was asked to do something, anything, by Diane. In a piece of work with another professional, Diane had been coached in using reward-punishment strategies: being firm and consistent with her instructions, praising Kayla when she followed instructions and ignoring Kayla when she was having a rage outburst. Diane had tried very hard with these strategies but found the escalation of Kayla's rage, for example, hitting and kicking Diane and screaming until the neighbours complained, impossible to ignore. Concerns were being raised about Diane's willingness to work with professionals and her ability to follow through with the reward-punishment strategies that she had been advised to use in response to Kayla's rage. All of the adults were becoming frustrated because, after two years of work, Kayla's rage outbursts had not decreased at all.

I observed one of Kayla's rage outbursts the first time that I met her. It was at the end of the session when Diane had asked Kayla, assertively but not harshly, to put on her coat as the session was ending. Kayla resisted and Diane followed through in accordance with the reward-punishment strategies she'd been taught. She calmly persisted with the instruction, though looked extremely anxious, and then went to put Kayla's coat on for her. Kayla screamed with disproportionate volume, switching between looking angry and smiling; however, there was little doubt that she was extraordinarily distressed. Kayla responded to her carer's approach by backing up against the wall, continuing to scream her lungs out and banging her head, hard, against the brick wall behind her.

Sarah

I've talked a little about Sarah and her two long-term foster carers, Simon and Rachel, in Chapter 1. Sarah was a loving, intelligent seven-year-old girl. She had lived with her mother and, variously, her father and her mother's partner. It is thought that there is likely to have been domestic violence between her mother and her mother's two partners. Sarah was passed around several of her family members, to live with them for days, weeks or months at a time, when her mother could not cope. After the local authority became involved Sarah was placed with her grandmother; however, when she was 18 months old, this placement broke down, at which time she moved to live with Simon and Rachel.

The rage outburst that I saw from Sarah was a week after one of her quarterly contacts with her father and two days after her birthday. Simon had reported that Sarah appeared to have had very positive contact with her father and that they had had fun together. Sarah reportedly came home happy and talked lots about the time she had spent with her father. Simon also explained that her birthday had gone very well; she had had a sleep-over with several of her friends, and members of the carers' family had visited her and brought cards and presents. Unfortunately, her father had not, as he had promised, sent Sarah a card or present for her birthday. Rachel had told me that Sarah hadn't seemed to notice and hadn't mentioned it.

Approximately 15 minutes before the end of my session with Sarah and her foster family, Sarah asked Simon to sit a little differently on the floor so that she could sit on his knee. He moved slightly and indicated his willingness to have Sarah sit on his lap. Sarah then started to scream and shout at Simon because he hadn't moved his legs enough. Simon and Rachel encouraged Sarah to sit down and explained that Simon couldn't move any more and still be comfortable. Sarah quickly escalated into a rage outburst; she cried, screamed, made to hit her carers and finally went to sit in the bathroom where she threw things around, ultimately breaking a glass bottle of bubble bath.

Simon and Rachel initially responded to Sarah's rage outburst by reiterating the reason that Simon couldn't move his legs as she had wanted him to but eventually they became irritated by Sarah's allegations that Simon didn't want her to sit on his knee. Sarah's allegations then escalated; she told her carers that they were always mean to her, that they didn't like her and then, when Rachel tried to touch her gently, that Rachel had hit her. Rachel and Simon responded to the various accusations that Sarah made with understandable annoyance and rational logic, that is, 'I asked you to sit on my knee! So why on earth do you think that I don't want you to?', 'I didn't hit you, Sarah!' They also reacted to her provocative, dangerous behaviours with reward-punishment thinking, that is, in a firm, raised voice, 'do not throw that, Sarah!', and interventive behaviour, for example, when Sarah raised a hand to Simon he held her arm so that she could not hit him. When Sarah retreated to the bathroom, before she started to break things, the carers talked with each other in angry, exasperated voices about how impossible Sarah was to care for.

In Kayla's and Sarah's cases the carers explained to me that the accounts above were typical of the children's rage outbursts. They also described, independently, that typically, after such outbursts, each of the girls would return to being happy and back to normal at a speed they found irritating and alarming.

Kevin

Kevin was a ten-year-old boy who lived with his adoptive parents, Sue and Joe, and his three younger birth siblings. Prior to being removed from his birth family Kevin had been exposed to frequent episodes of extremely violent domestic abuse and the physical abuse of both him and his siblings. In addition, due to the emotional vulnerability and mental health difficulties of his mother, he had also acted in many ways as parent and protector to her and his siblings.

Sue recounted one of Kevin's worst rage outbursts. On the evening before the rage took hold, Kevin had been sat next to Sue on the sofa as the family watched a film together. Kevin had moved very close to Sue on the sofa and Sue, feeling in need of some space, had asked him to move along the sofa a little.

The following day Sue had overheard Kevin in the next room talking to his six-year-old sister, telling her to 'go and get my trainers or else'. Sue responded by going to speak to Kevin about what he had said. She asked them both what was going on and, when neither was forthcoming with information, Sue had told Kevin, in a firm, calm voice, that he should not speak to his sister in that way and that if he wanted his trainers he should get them himself. As Sue walked away she heard Kevin say 'Fuck off, stupid bitch!' Sue went back into the room and asked him, with a raised, angry voice, what he had said; she shouted at him not to swear at her and then sent him to his room.

After 20 minutes Sue went up to see Kevin in his room to discuss the issue. Rather than calming down, as Sue had hoped, Kevin had become even angrier. As soon as he saw her he moved to the back edge of his top bunk and screamed, swore and shouted at her to get out of his room. Sue carried on trying to assert herself with Kevin, approaching as she reprimanded him. As she came closer Kevin started flailing his arms and legs from his position on the bed so that he kicked and hit her. Sue described Kevin as being 'like a wild animal' and that she felt compelled to restrain him in order to prevent him from hurting himself. As she did this she also called for one of the other children to get her adult son, Darren, who lived on the same street.

When Darren arrived he went into the bedroom and shouted at Kevin, 'What the hell do you think you're doing? If you ever hurt my mum again you'll regret it!' Sue explained to me that as Darren said this the muscles in Kevin's body 'just seemed to relax and he dropped'.

Later Kevin was beside himself, hysterical with regret and shame over what he had done and desperate to apologise to his adoptive mother. He told her that he was a horrible boy, that he didn't blame her for not loving him any more and he then tried to help her by getting involved in every household task he could think of. Within an hour Kevin had gone into his room and had fallen fast asleep on his bed. When Sue talked to him about how aggressive he had been with her he said that he couldn't remember any of it.

Typical reward-punishment strategies for rage outbursts

As demonstrated in the examples above, it is common for carers instinctively to use reward-punishment thinking in the heat of the moment of a rage outburst. It is, after all, the method that adults are relentlessly encouraged to use with children's 'bad' behaviour.

Kayla's carer, Diane, focused on Kayla's behaviour and tried very hard to implement consistent, uncompromising instructions that did not alter in the face of her protest. Diane also used a physical intervention to reinforce the boundary she had set, i.e. going to put Kayla's coat on for her.

Sarah's carers, Simon and Rachel, tried to discourage Sarah's 'bad' behaviour by various reward-punishment strategies including raising their voices to deter her behaviour. They also paid attention only to the verbal messages that Sarah gave rather than using her non-verbal information to understand Sarah's state of mind. They also, understandably, reacted defensively to her allegations against them by denying her allegations.

In the case of Kevin, Sue responded to Kevin's rage outburst by applying personal space boundaries, using a raised voice and sending Kevin to his room to deter the undesirable behaviour. Finally, Sue's adult son, Darren resorted to physical threat in an attempt to make Kevin's dangerous behaviour less likely to be repeated.

In all of these examples the carers reacted instinctively to their child's emotional messages rather than understanding what the emotional messages meant, that is, by becoming angry, frightened and/or feeling hopeless. The result was that the situations were all dominated and driven by emotions, and yet, in each example, the focus was on the behaviour. The emotions of the interaction were pushed entirely to the periphery yet it was these emotions that had driven the conflict.

The emotions and behaviour of developmentally traumatised children will often be very inconsistent due to a lack of empathy for the child's emotions in their infancy. During the rage outbursts of such children, possibly the most emotionally provocative problem behaviour that we see, it is crucial to be able to acknowledge and work with the emotions and behaviours simultaneously.

Making sense of rage outbursts

The most important elements to think about, from the EBM model (Figure 4.1), when seeking to understand the rage outbursts of developmentally traumatised children are hard-wired survival strategies, the effects of experience on brain and biology, emotional regulation, trauma memory and shame (in bold).

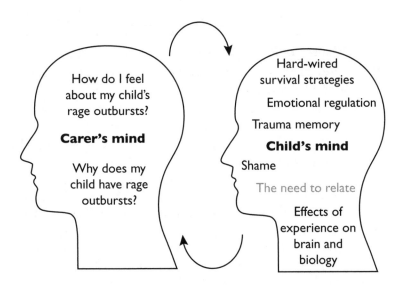

Figure 4.1 EBM model of rage outbursts

Hard-wired survival strategies

Invariably, when children react with extreme anger, they are responding in accordance with their own fear. Fear, in this case, is not just fear of physical harm but also fear of abandonment, rejection, criticism, etc. A rage outburst is a response to cues in the child's environment that they are in physical and/or emotional danger. The ability to pick up on such cues and the ability to switch into behaving aggressively, like a wild animal even, have provided an invaluable mechanism for improving the child's safety.

The triggers for rage outbursts, when children are in safe homes, are not typically those things that adults understand to be frightening. This is because such children learn to pre-empt and therefore react before the frightening event. If children had waited for the overtly frightening behaviour to begin, then they would have given themselves very little time in which to make themselves safe. Therefore children who have been exposed to prolonged periods of fear have learned to read and interpret the nuances of their environment, and the behaviour of the adults around them, in a manner that will give them the maximum possible time to react. There are many types of experience that can lead to fear in infancy (see Box 4.1).

Box 4.1 Causes of fear in babies

Prolonged exposure to any of the following can cause atypical cortisol levels and thus alter brain development in infants:

- *Neglect*: Infants need the constant availability of a carer; consequently the absence of responsive care can be very frightening for a baby.
- *Physical abuse*: Being physically hurt by an adult is, of course, frightening for anyone but it is terrifying for a baby.
- *Rough handling*: e.g. over-enthusiastic play, insensitive, careless handling. The way a baby is touched and held, if it is not responsive to a child's cues about what they can tolerate, may be frightening for an infant.
- *The anger/fear of others*: e.g. domestic abuse. Other people being frightened in the proximity of a baby will mean that they are less responsive to the infant. In addition, when dealing with their own distress they will be much less able to contain the distress of the baby. They may also behave in a way that is frightening to the baby, e.g. screaming, shouting, throwing objects, slamming doors, sudden movements.

It is important to consider that all of the above applies not only to the behaviour of adults but also the behaviour of other children. In environments in which older children are not supervised their behaviour may be causing fear to their infant sibling.

Control has also often played a significant role, in the early lives of traumatised children, in keeping them safe in frightening situations (this is thoroughly explored in Chapter 7). Therefore taking control away from a traumatised child (e.g. limit setting, boundaries) may also induce fear. As adults, of course, we are unlikely instinctively to consider that something as innocuous as saying 'no' to a third chocolate biscuit could possibly induce fear; however, it can often be the case. Maintaining control will have been an integral part of enabling the child's safety in very frightening environments in their past. Therefore any attempt to parent effectively can be perceived, by children who have experienced fear in early life, as an attempt to place them in a vulnerable position.

Rage outbursts can also be triggered by commonplace parent-child confrontations. If this is the case then it can indicate that the child has an unconscious conviction that any parent-child conflict is potentially very dangerous and fear inducing.

The effects of experience on brain and biology

A child's prolonged exposure to their own fear impacts on the development of their brain, in particular the way in which the stress hormone, cortisol, is processed. This atypical physiological reaction to cortisol means that rage outbursts are more likely to be triggered in times of stress.

Babies who have prolonged exposure to danger, and therefore fear, produce excessive amounts of cortisol. There are then two possible ways in which the brain can respond. The child's brain can do nothing with the cortisol except to go about processing it in the best way it can; alternatively, the brain can shut down some of the cortisol receptors so that the child's brain responds less to the cortisol.

There is currently some argument among scientists about the way in which these two responses impact on children's behaviour. However, one of the strongest theories suggests that the brain of a traumatised child is not fixed in its response to cortisol but that it is performing a constant balancing exercise between the two methods (Mason *et al.* 2001).

There is some evidence to suggest that most of the children who have rage outbursts have low levels of cortisol (therefore many of their cortisol receptors will have shut down) rather than the higher levels one might expect (McBurnett *et al.* 2000). This makes sense if we understand that such children may be quite emotionally avoidant and that their attempts to repress their emotions may cause a rebound effect, forcing their rage to vent in one big explosion rather than being released gradually over time.

Research also suggests that children who have had prolonged experience of fear and violence tend to perceive violent intent, and the potential for aggression, in more situations than other children. Rage outbursts may, therefore, be caused by hypersensitivity to aggression and misinterpretation of facial expression and tone of voice (Dejonghe *et al.* 2005).

Emotional regulation

Understanding the difficulties that developmentally traumatised children have with regulating their emotions can add a great deal to our interpretation of their rage outbursts (remember the toilet training analogy in Chapter 1). If a child does not have any internal or external means by which to moderate their own emotional reactions then these are likely to be extreme; the emotional thermostat of such children is likely to have a very limited range, that is, either 'on' or 'off'.

It can be useful to think of a rage outburst of a developmentally traumatised child as equivalent to a baby's cry but with the addition of greater physicality and the ability to talk about the mechanics of the outburst. Both are expressions of extreme distress unmitigated by, and disconnected from, any understanding of their distress and how to overcome it.

Generally, we expect that children should be able both to account for the reasons behind their 'anger' and attempt to control it. The child's understanding of adult expectations, coupled with their disconnection from the nature and cause of their distress, often results in the child coming up with a rationale for their rage, for example, 'You're always horrible to me!'. The rationale at that stage is unlikely to be accurate but it might well meet adult expectations, even though we may not accept the child's explanation. It is for this reason that such a child will often produce, when asked, an inaccurate but, on some level, sensible explanation for her behaviour, for example Sarah's assertion that Rachel had hit her. If it were true, this rationale would indeed have made sense of Sarah's extreme distress.

In addition, children will often internalise an understanding of their rage outbursts using the logic of the world around them. Instead of understanding their own legitimate feelings of rage, children who have rage outbursts will invariably believe that the rage demonstrates their 'real' inherently 'bad' selves. It is for this reason that one of the most important aspects of parenting such children is to ensure that you acknowledge your child's legitimate distress and reconnect it with its actual cause.

Trauma memory and shame

Trauma memory and shame are also implicated in rage outbursts. Children often won't remember their rage outburst because under stress their brain will process events in a sensory way (see Chapter 1). This means that these memories are not verbally accessible and so cannot be understood in an organised way and certainly not in a way that can be spoken about. As you can see in the description of Kevin's rage outburst, his inability to control his behaviour, in combination with the use of reward-punishment strategies, designed to convey to him that it should be controllable, led to his consequent shame and self-loathing about this traumatised element of his character.

It is important to understand that rage is a very sensible reaction to fear and in the case of developmentally traumatised children, fear caused by anger, rejection and/or abandonment. It is therefore understandable that children make associations between rage and their previous experiences and react to things that previously warranted it.

Rage outbursts and you

Rage outbursts are perhaps the most difficult type of behaviour that carers of developmentally traumatised children have to deal with. They often invoke some very challenging feelings in carers (and professionals) such as anger, irritation, hopelessness, helplessness, frustration, disheartenment, a feeling of being overwhelmed, fear, intimidation, rejection, etc. Rage outbursts are so immediate and urgent that they can also disable carers' ability to stop and think about how to respond, which leaves them only with their instinctive reactions (Boxes 4.2 and 4.3).

As with many of the typical behaviours brought on by early abuse and/or neglect, carers may feel, on some level, as though their child's rage outbursts are deliberate and nasty attempts to control and manipulate rather than the infantile reactions to their experiences.

Due to the power of rage outbursts and the reaction they can provoke in carers it is extremely important that they fully explore the 'EBM for carers' strategies to prevent the buttons that are pressed turning into undesirable methods of parenting.

Box 4.2 Relationship replication: hyperarousal
Birth family experience

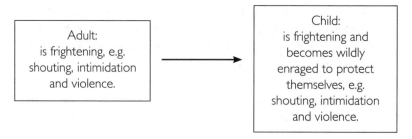

The parent behaves in a way that is persistently/unpredictably frightening for the child, for example, shouting, being intimidating and/or violent. The child's fear reaction becomes hyper-reactive and so they react aggressively to any hint of aggression in order to protect themselves, for example, by shouting, being intimidating and/or violent.

Foster/Adoptive family experience

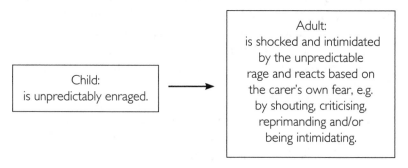

The child's fear reaction is hypersensitive and so uses the unconscious strategy of defaulting to rage when frightened. The child therefore reacts aggressively to any hint of aggression, e.g. shouting, reprimand or criticism, in order to protect from a perceived attack. The carer is taken by surprise by the unpredictable aggression, feels intimidated and so reacts based on their own fear by shouting, intimidating, criticising and/or shaming the child.

SUMMARY: The frightening parenting has caused the child to be hyper-reactive to threat. The child has unconsciously invited the carer to frighten them. The carer has accepted the invitation.

Box 4.3 Relationship replication: emotional regulation

Birth family experience

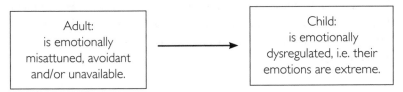

The parent is neither emotionally available nor able to regulate the emotions of their child and so the child does not learn how to regulate themselves. Consequently all of the child's emotional reactions are heightened, extreme and frightening.

Foster/Adoptive family experience

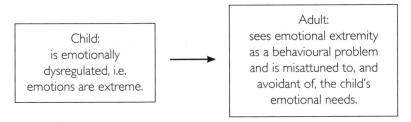

The child is emotionally dysregulated, that is, their emotions are extreme, volatile, unpredictable, irrational and challenging. The carer feels overwhelmed by the emotional and behavioural intensity and so avoids, or is unable to see, the emotional distress that underlies the emotional volatility.

SUMMARY: The misattuned parenting has caused the child to develop extreme emotional reactions. The child has unconsciously invited the carer not to regulate the child's emotions or engage with them on an emotional level. The carer has accepted the invitation.

Consequences of not responding empathically to rage outbursts

We have explored the logic of rage outbursts and how they make sense as reactions to children's early trauma. I have also given examples of the typical ways in which rage outbursts are often dealt with both instinctively and by using reward-punishment strategies rather than those driven by empathy.

It is useful to consider the implications of using reward-punishment thinking in response to the rage outbursts of developmentally traumatised children. I have already alluded to some of the potential consequences, but for a more thorough list see Box 4.4.

Box 4.4 The effect of not responding empathically to rage outbursts

When the rage outbursts of developmentally traumatised children are managed with reward-punishment thinking, that is, without understanding how the outbursts make sense and without empathy for their cause, there are consequences for children's emotional and psychological health.

- Continued rage outbursts into adulthood. The child never learns to regulate their emotions and so carries this difficulty into adulthood.
- Low self-esteem. The lack of understanding and control of their own behaviour leads to shame and self-blame, which results in poor self-esteem.
- Depression. The child's lack of empathy for themselves leads to self-judgement and potentially a depressive presentation.
- Self-harm. This can be a successful way of managing emotions in the absence of an internal regulatory process developed via interpersonal relationships.
- Dissociative disorders. The continued inability to regulate emotions will necessitate the need to opt out psychologically. This can take the form of dissociative disorders.
- Psychotic symptoms (e.g. hallucinations and delusions). The separation of 'perceived reality', that is, extreme distress, and 'understood/narrative reality', that is, no apparent logical cause for the distress, can result in a psychological experience of multiple realities.

Empathic behaviour management strategies: rage outbursts

EBM for carers

RESPONSIVE EBM FOR CARERS

Rage outbursts often spark one of the most powerful invitations to react instinctively to the behaviour of our children. Being faced with unpredictable aggression encourages people to disengage the rational frontal lobes of their brains in order for them to use the more primitive, survival-related parts of their brains. It is therefore important for carers to prepare for the possibility of rage outbursts by reading the first two chapters of this book and by using the exercises there to develop their self-awareness. This will help carers to calm the primitive parts of their brains and enable them to re-engage the more controllable, rational parts of their brain.

Human biology, in the face of unpredictable rage, provokes impulsive, angry, aggressive reactions and, whilst it is important to notice these reactions and their impact on parenting, the emotions created in carers will not pass unless they apply an empathic approach to themselves. In short, it is, of course, absolutely fine to feel angry, hopeless, helpless, etc. but it can be useful to understand these emotions as invitations to behave in a certain way rather than as inevitable parenting dead ends.

The important thing for carers to remember is that they should not try to deny their emotional reactions either to themselves or to their children. It is useful for carers to try to make sense of them, so that they can help their children to do the same. Any attempt to deny or completely mask carers' reactions will only lead to disingenuous communications and further emotional disorientation for the child. In short, carers should aim to keep their verbal and non-verbal communications consistent and to be empathic to the emotion that has caused their child's rage outburst.

PREVENTATIVE EBM FOR CARERS

Externalising the rage outbursts (carer only)

The idea behind this technique is to see the problem as an entirely separate entity from the child; it allows carers to examine and interrogate the rage outbursts without allowing their negative feelings about them to dominate their relationship with their child.

The first step for carers is to decide what they will call the outbursts. They should be given a name that feels like it encapsulates them in some way that is right for the carer. They could be called the Rage, the Outbursts, the Meltdowns, etc. Or carers can be far more creative and name them after some distinctive feature that rings true for them, for example, Scary Eyes or the Wild Animal.

When carers have named the rage outbursts they can then find a way to represent them. Carers might like to draw the outbursts as a person, creature or a scene. Alternatively, carers who don't feel particularly artistic could write a story about their externalised rage character. Whatever carers do, the outburst should be personified in some way that enables them to keep the outbursts separate in their mind from their child or any real person.

Having externalised the rage, carers can start trying to understand it using the following techniques. Carers might like to write a letter to the externalised problem (Box 4.5) or write a survey for the problem character to fill in. In their letter carers can rant at the problem, really tell it how it makes them feel. They can ask it questions such as 'Where did you come from?' 'What do you like?', etc. Care should be taken not to address the letter to the child; carers should write to a fictional character that represents the rage that inhabits their child.

Box 4.5 Letter to the Rage

To the Rage,

Right you, I've had enough! I'm sick of the control you have over me and my family. How dare you! You've come into my home and upset and frightened everybody. You're a bully and I'm going to stand up to you.

Let me tell you a little bit about what you have done.

When you get inside Peter it's like you take him over.

My daughter, Jessica, has got exams at the moment and yesterday, when you made Peter kick off about what we were going to have for dinner, you ruined her whole evening of revision and she needs to revise!

As for me, you're making my life a misery! I've turned into this snappy, short-tempered person that I never used to be until you got here!

Even the dog hates you and she loves everyone!

And what about Peter? Well, when you're not around he can be such a kind, lovely boy. He helps with the dishes, he plays nicely with his friends. But when you get your claws into him, you turn him into a wild animal! You make him hit, kick and spit at me. You even make him hurt himself sometimes when he's flailing around because you've made him lose it. And then you even have the audacity to make him feel guilty when you've finished with him and we all have to pick up the pieces.

So go on, tell me why. Tell me why you do it, what do you get out of it? What's so good about coming into our home and ruining things for everyone? What is it you like about our house and living inside Peter in particular?

Yours sincerely

Annabel, Peter's mum.

After carers have written to the externalised rage character, it is useful for them to take a break and then write back to themselves taking on the role of the rage character (Box 4.6). It is important for carers to suspend their own feelings about the problem and to make sure that they avoid the temptation to write back to themselves as though they are writing from their child. Carers should try very hard to imagine that they are this fictional character that embodies the outbursts.

Box 4.6 Letter from the Rage

Dear Annabel,

Well, it's nice to finally hear from you. I wondered when you were going to try to have a chat with me directly rather than trying to get Peter to do all the work.

Frankly, you've made me a very nice little home in your house. I love it when you shout at Peter and send him to his room when I've been pulling his strings. That only gives me more control of Peter and then I can really get him to let rip!

The thing is, Annabel, Peter and I have known each other far longer than he has known you. Have you ever considered that I might actually have been a good friend to Peter in the past? Imagine what a pathetic creature he would have been if I wasn't around when his father was knocking his mother's teeth out, doing his best to do the same to Peter or when his mother kicked him outside when Peter dared to complain to her about it.

As a good friend, I'm certainly not going to abandon Peter now, just because you say that you're not going to do the same as his dad did. In fact, the other day, when I got Peter to smash your precious photo frame, you looked pretty close to hurting Peter yourself. You see why he still needs me?

As a result, while Peter is still in potential danger, I'll be sticking around. On the other hand if you think that you can persuade Peter to feel safe with you, that he doesn't need me any more, then maybe I can have a bit of a break from time to time. To be honest though, I think the idea of trusting anyone but me will be a pretty hard idea for him to believe in.

Kind regards

Your long-term house guest, the Rage.

Carers who are more comfortable expressing themselves in artistic ways could draw the externalised character and draw how the Rage can be calmed and prevented from having the power that it has over their child.

Carers might find it useful to use the adaptations to this exercise (below) to enable their child to join in with the externalisation; this may help carer and child to join forces against the rage outbursts.

Seeds of Truth exercise

The Seeds of Truth exercise is a way of understanding what the origin of a child's rage outburst is. It is important to accept that somewhere in the child's behaviour is the real story about their experiences but that unfortunately the child can't explain it directly; in fact, it is quite likely that they have no idea what it is themselves.

A rage outburst is a non-verbal communication from a child who is desperately trying to convey their internal experience via their behaviour. By directing the rage outburst at their carer the child implies that the carer is deserving of the rage, that is, the rage is an implied allegation that the carer has done something terrible to their child and this has provoked the child's rage.

In order to better understand the rage outbursts, carers may find the following questions useful:

- What is the allegation implied by your child when they direct their rage at you?
- Why, theoretically might you be deserving of the rage?

Is your child implying by their behaviour that:

- you have treated them badly?
- you have been unfair?
- you don't care about them?
- you are starving them?
- you have threatened them?
- you have hit them?
- you don't respond to their physical and/or emotional needs?
- you don't like them? etc.

After carers have answered these questions honestly, the next stage is to deal with any that might be factually accurate. Whilst it is unlikely that many of these will be true, there might be some. If there are then they must be approached with honesty and humility.

When this has been done carers can truly remove the temptation to take the implied allegation personally; their consciences can be clear: 'OK, so I genuinely know that I do love her and that I have not tried to starve her despite what she seems to be saying and feeling.' When this has been done carers can move on from the need to defend themselves and start to think about where the implied allegation *really* comes from, how it actually makes sense. Carers might find the following questions helpful in making sense of this.

- Is the implied allegation accurate but simply directed towards the wrong person? Perhaps someone from your child's past?
- Where could the feeling inherent in the allegation, e.g. loneliness, fear of not being looked after, fear that you don't care about her, come from? Are these feelings that your child is very familiar with?
- Might something in your behaviour, facial expression, tone of voice, etc. have been misconstrued by your child and provoked negative feelings in them, from their past?

Having worked through these stages carers can use this understanding of the legitimate cause of their child's rage in their empathic commentary (below) with their child. Carers can share with their child that they have some ideas about where the rage, worry or fear has come from. Carers can help the child to explore, without blame, the ways in which their rage makes absolute sense as a consequence of their past experiences. Carers can help their children to make sense of why the rage has been expressed in the relationship between the two of them because something reminded the child of a horrible feeling from their past.

EBM for children
RESPONSIVE EBM FOR CHILDREN
Empathic commentary
It is useful when employing this strategy to refer back to the Golden Rules of empathic commentary (Box 3.9 in Chapter 3).

Carers will typically need to use empathic commentary statements in response to their child's rage outbursts, quite relentlessly and for a prolonged period of time. If possible it can be useful to take shifts with someone else who understands the strategy and who the child trusts. This can help to prevent the insidious, but very understandable, effects of carers' negative feelings about the rage outbursts on their parenting.

It can also be useful, when parenting a child who has rage outbursts, to empathise with not only the feeling that has caused the outburst but also the fear that children often experience about their own confusion and lack of control.

When using empathic commentary with rage outbursts (Box 4.7) it is important that carers pay close attention to their voice and body language and not just the content of what they say. Carers will need to match the urgency and tone of their child's tone of voice. However, for carers to mirror the child's rage in their voice they require a very empathic, open facial expression, in order to convey clearly that they are empathic to, rather than angry with, their child.

Box 4.7 Responsive empathic commentary for rage outbursts

The following are some examples of the empathic commentary that carers can use during rage outbursts to help children to manage their intense feelings. The following statements can be used as a starting point but carers should feel free to come up with their own.

- 'You're so angry.'
- 'It really feels like I'm being mean to you at the moment. I'm so sorry.'
- 'I'm so sorry that I couldn't let you have another biscuit. I think it reminded you of when you didn't have control of what you ate and Mummy didn't give you enough food.'
- 'It all feels so overwhelming to you at the moment. I really want to work hard at making things feel better.'
- 'You must be so scared to get so angry. I wonder what it is that is feeling so frightening to you.'
- 'Me saying, "no" has made you so angry with me. I think it reminds you of when things were so frightening with Dad. I'm so sorry that he made you that scared.'
- 'Oh my, you're really angry at me all of a sudden and it really feels like it's about me being horrible to you.'
- 'Wow, it really feels like I actually hit you! That must be so scary! I really want to keep you safe.'
- 'No wonder you've jumped to defend yourself by being angry. You're used to having to protect yourself from grown-ups who hurt you in the past!'

Rhythmical calming

Carers may find that it is possible, during a rage outburst, to redirect their child to a rhythmical activity. To understand why *rhythmical calming* works just think about what is instinctively done for babies when they are distressed (think back to the baby's cry exercise in Box 3.1, Chapter 3). The instinct is to rock them, bounce them, touch them and talk melodically and rhythmically. Rhythmical calming is a way of replicating this with an older child who is experiencing similar levels of dysregulated distress, that is, having a rage outburst.

The ideal method of rhythmical calming would be to rock the child or stroke their skin rhythmically, just like with a baby. However, it is important to consider whether the child may misinterpret your touch, particularly if their rage outburst relates to a memory of physical or sexual abuse. Carers will be able to make a judgement on how this may be perceived based on their research into their child's history and by using a tentative approach. If children have had experiences such as these then rhythmical calming can still be attempted but tentatively to gauge the child's level of comfort.

It might be challenging for carers to talk their child into doing these activities whilst they are in the midst of a rage outburst but it is often most effective for carers to start the activity themselves and encourage their child to join them. There is something surprisingly enticing about rhythm for all of us when we're feeling out of control so carers can often be surprised by their child's enthusiasm for rhythmical calming activities (Box 4.8).

Box 4.8 Rhythmical calming

The following are examples of rhythmical calming that carers might like to try as a method of diverting their child into a calming activity when they are in the middle of a rage outburst.

- Jumping up and down.
- Hopping.
- Marching.
- Counting loudly.
- Clapping your hands.
- Using a punch bag using a simple pattern of punches.
- Slapping a pillow.
- Banging drum.
- Singing/chanting/shouting nursery rhymes/songs.

Carers are an essential part of enabling their children to calm, so carers should not send their child away to use these exercises; they can do the activity with their child and perhaps use some empathic commentary too.

Rhythmical calming can be used as a preventative strategy as well as a responsive one. Using rhythmical calming when children are already calm can help them to learn some emotional regulation skills that they can apply for themselves when they have strong emotions to manage in the future.

PREVENTATIVE EBM FOR CHILDREN

The main skill that we are trying to develop in children who experience rage outbursts is an ability to regulate their emotions. Developmentally traumatised children have more challenging emotions to manage than most people and they have been afforded the least nurturing environments in which to develop such regulatory skills. Therefore carers' main focus should be to enable their children to regulate their own emotions by doing it for them first. The following are ways for carers to help their children to develop these skills and thus are ways of preventing the child's vulnerability to rage outbursts in the long-term.

Preventative empathic commentary

Carers can use empathic commentary statements in calm times to give their children feedback about what they are experiencing internally (remember the toilet training analogy in Chapter 1). Carers shouldn't feel restricted to using empathic commentary only in times of stress; in fact it is very helpful to use it at times when things are much more settled and happy. All carers need to do is notice, out loud, the things that they think are going on in their child's mind and body (Box 4.9).

Imagine that the emotional thermostat of a child who has rage outbursts only has the 'on' and 'off' settings. Giving the child feedback, about the tiny nuances of their internal experience, helps them to develop the full 1 to 10 range on their thermostat. In addition to using empathic commentary, carers can help to improve their child's emotional range by getting into the habit of reflecting the child's emotions back to them with the carer's facial expressions and body language.

Box 4.9 Preventative empathic commentary for rage outbursts

These are some examples of the empathic commentary that carers can use in calm periods to prevent rage. These are a starting point but carers should feel free to come up with their own.

- 'Gosh, you're very excited! It's so hard for you to control your excitement; no wonder that's something babies usefully learn to from their parents doing for them when they're tiny.'
- 'I think maybe you're feeling a bit sad today because you and Jess fell out at school yesterday.'
- 'Sometimes it's hard for you to stop the excitement turning into fighting.'
- 'Ooh, you're really enjoying your breakfast this morning.'
- 'You look so happy when you play with Nitesh on the trampoline!'
- 'Running fast feels really good, doesn't it?'
- 'Oh dear, that was annoying for you.'

Externalise the rage outbursts (carer and child)

Carers can extend the externalisation exercise (above) to involve their child. The objective is to help the child to create a character that represents their rage outbursts. The character the child creates can be entirely different from the character that the carer created in the exercise above. The child can draw the character or write to it or the carer and child could even play a game whereby the carer plays the role of the rage character and their child could interview them as if they are the rage.

No matter who does this exercise the key is that it should enable whoever does it to separate the problem from the child so that the problem can be combated without losing empathy for the child.

Head Weather

The objective of *Head Weather* is to help carer and child to communicate about their feelings routinely. They will both talk about them as a regular part of the day just like they might discuss the weather.

The first stage is to prepare the materials that will be used. Carers will already have a good idea about the range of their child's emotional language and understanding but carer and child should sit down together and talk about what emotions the child knows and understands. If they have a very limited emotional vocabulary then carers can use *Mind–Mood Connections* (below) as an alternative to Head Weather.

Working together, the carer and child can make symbols for each of the emotions that the child knows and understands. The amount of emotions might be very limited in the beginning but it should grow as time goes on. Carers should also make a 'days of the week' chart with a row for each person in the house and a column for each day of the week. Towards the end of each day the household can come together and each person should use the relevant emotion symbol to explain how they have felt during the day.

For older children it might be more effective to use a post box or for carers to encourage their child to give them a symbol or a note in order to make the communication more personal and private. If the child can tolerate using this method of communication as a way to initiate a conversation with their carer about their feelings then that's even better. It is important to remember, however, that it can be very surprising just how well teenagers, who have experienced early trauma, respond to 'young child' activities. It is frequently the case that adults' worries and self-consciousness prevent the attempt to engage older children in trying these playful activities.

Mind–Mood Connections

Mind–Mood Connections is an alternative to Head Weather for children who have a very limited emotional vocabulary. After using this strategy for a while carers may feel able to move on to Head Weather but any transition should be taken at the child's pace and carers should try to resist the pressure to rush.

The Mind–Mood Connections technique is simply employing the Head Weather format, but instead of the child having to choose an emotion symbol for themselves their carer can do it for them by 'reading' their mood. The technique could be made even more playful by the carer pretending to be a mind-reader or a magician.

Carers can make a game of reading their child's emotions at the end of the day and telling the child, tentatively, how they think the child feels. This helps because carers are making the connections between their child's internal experiences and appropriate emotion words for them. Head Weather can still be used for the rest of the family as it will model to the child how other people understand their own internal worlds and regulate their emotions, and it can help to normalise difficult emotions.

Box 4.10 Things to remember about rage outbursts

Understanding how rage outbursts make sense

- Rage outbursts are invariably adaptive strategies developed in response to a child's previous experience. Your child may have been in situations in which the red mist has very much helped them to stay safe.

- Prolonged experience of fear in infancy leads children to see the potential for violence more often than other children, so a rage outburst may be triggered by fear of this perceived aggression.

- Prolonged fear also alters the way in which the stress hormone cortisol is produced and disposed of, often leading to explosive anger.

- Children who have experienced abuse and/or neglect have greater difficulties in understanding and regulating their emotions. Their emotional thermostat can be limited to the 'on' and 'off' settings.

- Rage outbursts are often dissociative, i.e. the child's conscious mind is not active and so when they say they do not remember the rage outbursts they are likely to be telling the truth.

- Traumatised children's genuine lack of control of the rage outbursts, combined with their difficulty in dealing with shame, can leave them unable to deal with the resultant damage to their relationship with their carer(s).

- Rage outbursts can be the hardest behaviour for a carer to respond empathically to, as they can be intimidating, overwhelming and frightening.

Understanding what to do

- EBM for carers:
  - Responsive strategies:
    - A good understanding for a carer of what their own emotional reactions are likely to be can help them to be calmer and less judgemental of their own reactions.
    - Carers should not try to deny or mask their feelings but understand them and work with them.
  - Preventative strategies:
    - Carers can benefit from developing an awareness of their own reactions to rage outbursts.
    - Externalising the rage outbursts (carers only).
    - Seeds of Truth exercise.

- EBM for children:
  - Responsive strategies:
    - Responsive empathic commentary for rage outbursts.
    - Rhythmical calming.
  - Preventative strategies:
    - Preventative empathic commentary for rage outbursts.
    - Externalising the rage outbursts (carer and child).
    - Head Weather.
    - Mind–Mood Connections.

CHAPTER 5

The Girl in a Bubble

Introduction to the 'zoning out' phenomenon

Whilst it is rarely the biggest issue that foster carers and adoptive parents seek help with, 'zoning out' is a very common, but often only casually remarked upon, phenomenon seen in children traumatised by abuse and/or neglect. Zoning out is also often coupled with rage outbursts (discussed in Chapter 4).

Children who have zoned out are, typically, very difficult to rouse even by loud noises or physical contact. These episodes can look like a type of epileptic seizure (specifically absence seizures). It is important therefore that, if a child displays the symptoms that I will go on to describe, they should be taken for a medical examination to rule out the possibility of epileptic absence seizures.

If medical causes have been ruled out then the zoning out, in a developmentally traumatised child, might well be due to a dissociative absence. These absences are a psychological defence mechanism that allows a child to mentally distance themselves from dangerous situations in which they have learned that they are powerless (Perry 1997; Schore 2001). Dissociative episodes, or zoning out, are a powerful example of the way in which early trauma can impact profoundly on brain function.

There are, of course, degrees of zoning out, as demonstrated in the examples below. In some children it will be barely noticeable and they will come round very quickly but in others it can be more extreme and, seemingly, a default strategy for dealing with any experience that is outside their immediate comfort zone.

What is zoning out?

Misha

Misha was a 14-year-old girl who had lived with her long-term foster carers for two years. She had been severely neglected whilst living with her mother, during which time she was left locked alone in a bathroom for days at a time. Her mother suffered from severe depression and interacted with Misha very little. Misha had missed out on approximately two years of school. She had come into foster care aged 11.

Misha did not display any challenging behaviours but her carers and teachers were concerned because Misha appeared to interact on a very superficial level. She had learned to relate to some degree with her carers and teachers but when she was challenged or asked to do or think about anything that she didn't want to consider Misha would disappear into her 'bubble'.

When I met with Misha she was able to engage with artistic activities but when I introduced play activities and tried to talk with her, Misha froze and became like a statue. Her eyes would glaze over, she would stare into the middle distance and nothing that I did got any reaction from her. Misha simply disappeared.

Misha's carers and teachers had become quite frustrated with her and having tried encouragement, cajoling and discipline they had resorted to allowing Misha to engage only in those things that she chose to.

Both teachers and carers stated that Misha would come out of her bubble by herself, in her own time. When she did so she was unable to reflect upon where she had been and why she had disappeared, although this difficulty with reflection was quite typical for Misha. After coming out of her bubble Misha would be immediately back to her usual self.

Arun

Arun was a seven-year-old boy who had been adopted at 18 months. He had a history of witnessing domestic violence between his mother and father. He spent a great deal of time being cared for by his two older sisters who had fought over the right to play with him and handled him very roughly.

He had occasional rage outbursts, usually when his adoptive parents asked him to do something or when they said 'no' to him. His adoptive parents noticed that sometimes after a rage outburst, and sometimes instead of a rage outburst, Arun would go very quiet and be completely uncommunicative no matter what his parents did to get his attention. They described that these episodes would end when Arun eventually 'came around', that he would be completely back to normal again but that he would seemingly have no recollection of his 'absence'.

Arun's school had told his parents that he was performing below the average level for his age because he tended to daydream and struggled to concentrate.

Typical strategies

Carers can feel quite alarmed by their child zoning out, although they do not always seek help with the problem. Children who have developed this unconscious, physiological strategy are not necessarily challenging to manage in behavioural terms although carers can find that such children can be quite unsatisfying to look after.

As demonstrated in the previous examples, there is a danger that carers and/or teachers view children who zone out as daydreamers or as having attention problems. Consequently carers typically try to rouse their children as if they are daydreaming, perhaps even reaching the stage of shouting in annoyance to get their attention.

Whilst there is not typically a huge drive to use reward-punishment thinking explicitly, children who zone out can sometimes become labelled as lazy or inattentive and the frustration caused by their apparent failure to pay attention can cause disruption in their relationships, particularly with adults. This can cause carers to become inadvertently punitive, i.e. the irritation felt by carers can feel like a punishment to the child for their apparent lack of attention. In addition, children who dissociate can also be generally more dampened in their mood and their ability to relate to others (Cicchetti 1994) and so it can be more challenging to develop rewarding relationships with them.

The problem that arises when dissociative episodes are misunderstood is that the underlying problem is overlooked and consequently the need for a targeted strategy can be overlooked. This means that useful opportunities to enable a child to overcome the problem can be missed.

Making sense of zoning out

The crucial questions to ask ourselves when we are confronted with the presentation of a developmentally traumatised child that is challenging to understand are:

- 'What early childhood problem would this behaviour be a sensible or understandable solution to?'
- 'How is this behaviour a good solution to that problem?'

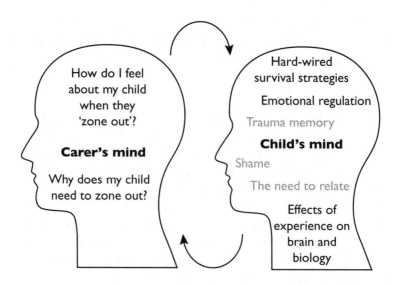

Figure 5.1 EBM model of dissociative episodes

The most important elements of the EBM model (Figure 5.1) to think about when seeking to understand a child's zoning out episodes are hard-wired survival strategies, emotional regulation and the effects of experience on brain and biology (in bold). The other factors cited in the EBM model are also influential, but to a lesser extent.

Hard-wired survival strategies and emotional regulation

Dissociative episodes are demonstrative of a complete inability to regulate difficult emotion. Such complete psychological shutdown is indicative that the child has found no other way in which to manage their emotions, that is, all of the typical ways that children effectively manage their emotions, even the problematic ways (e.g. rage outbursts, attention-seeking, controlling behaviour), have failed. Once such children have given up on any attempt to protect themselves physically, their only hope is to protect themselves psychologically; they do this by shutting down and creating complete psychological isolation.

Such extreme measures are usually a response to prolonged, extreme exposure to stress and fear, often when the child's object of love and protection is also their biggest object of fear.

The effects of experience on brain and biology

The neurological process of dissociative absences is not fully understood; however, they are thought to be related to the way in which a child's brain adapts to processing high levels of cortisol (stress hormone) in their infancy (Flack *et al.* 2000).

The process of metabolising excessive amounts of cortisol in traumatised children is also related to the biology which explains rage outbursts (Chapter 4); dissociative absences can often be the next neurochemical step after a rage outburst. Having produced such an enormous amount of physiological energy (including high levels of cortisol) with which to (unsuccessfully) deal with a threat, the next best solution, for a brain that has been well versed in dealing with large amounts of cortisol, is to shut down any ability to feel that threat (low cortisol) and induce a state of 'passive coping' (Flack *et al.* 2000).

When children are in a dissociative state their body calms, their heart rate decreases, regardless of what is going on around them, and, in more advanced stages of dissociation, the brain produces pain numbing opioids resulting in a reduced ability to feel pain, immobility and the inhibition of the urge to cry for help (Schore 2001). The child has turned their emotional thermostat to the 'off' position.

Overdoses of cortisol in early life, via prolonged exposure to stress/fear, creates in the brain the potential for a two-pronged approach to dealing with that stress/fear. First, the child's brain develops the ability to heighten its physical response, which might deter an attacker or enable the child to signal their desperate need for help. Second, if the first neurological strategy fails, and the danger is inescapable, it moves into a dissociative state in which the best a child's brain can do is tolerate physical harm by minimising the perception of the pain.

Those children who go straight into zoning out without having a rage outburst first are likely to have learned that the 'signalling for help' stage may actually make them more vulnerable, that is, crying or protesting may worsen their abuse.

We can conclude therefore that when a developmentally traumatised child goes into a dissociative state they have anticipated that something terribly frightening is likely to happen. It could be any number of things that might trigger this response; the cause can be as simple as detecting an emotional need or a need for assistance or support from their carer (see Box 5.1). Zoning out is therefore a very successful way for a child to remain, at a time of need, entirely separate from others, thereby preventing psychological vulnerability.

Box 5.1 Experiences that may cause children to zone out

There are many experiences that cause elevated cortisol levels in infancy that may leave a child sensitive to reminders of that experience and thus potentially lead a child to dissociate at times.

Early experience	Child's day to day reminder
Neglect	Experience of own emotions Hunger/thirst Waiting for food Tiredness Fear Pain Coldness Smell of cannabis Carer giving attention to someone else
Physical abuse/ domestic violence	Raised voices Going to bed Being separated from parent and/or sibling Parent/child conflict, including normal limit setting Sibling conflict Sound of keys in the front door Touch
Sexual abuse/ intrusive parenting	Bedtimes Presence of an unfamiliar adult Bath times Locked doors Touch
Critical parenting	Experience of not winning something competitive Carer giving attention to someone else
Any of the above	Sensory triggers, sights, sounds, smells, touches

Consequences of not responding empathically to zoning out

Adults frequently rationalise dissociation as poor attention, daydreaming and/or laziness. As a result it can lead carers to become irritated with their children who zone out. Carers can inadvertently punish a child who has dissociated by insisting that they stick with a task until they finish it, with the entirely benevolent aim of improving their child's attention span and focus. In addition, the therapeutic and educational needs of zoned-out children can frequently be missed as they do not typically pose many behavioural challenges.

Zoning out is an attempt, after all else has failed, to cope with frightening, overwhelming circumstances by passive coping, opting out and not feeling. Therefore any attempt to deal with this adaptive strategy as a problem behaviour without using empathy will, at best, be ineffective and, at worst, increase the child's need to retreat from their carer. Box 5.2 provides examples of the problems that can result from these approaches.

Box 5.2 The potential effects of not responding empathically to dissociation

When the dissociative episodes of developmentally traumatised children are managed with reward-punishment thinking, that is, without understanding how the phenomena make sense and without empathy for their cause, it can have a variety of impacts on children's well-being. Often these strategies will exacerbate the symptoms that co-occur with dissociative episodes.

- *Poor performance at school*: Not dealing with the cause of the dissociative episodes can increase a child's difficulties with managing their attention and concentration and thus damage their performance at school.

- *Rage outbursts*: Rage can provide a physiological release in times of dysregulated emotion and outbursts of rage often co-occur with dissociative episodes.

- *Social isolation and disengagement from society*: Children who have learned that interactions, in times of stress, are dangerous will have a tendency to isolate themselves. Adding more stress to this, via reward-punishment thinking, will increase the need to disengage.

- *Self-harm*: A child who has no concept of their own or others' ability to manage their emotions may seek physiological release from those emotions. This is a release that self-harm can provide.

- *Bizarre/atypical behaviours/beliefs*: A child who is out of touch with the social world around them may develop a fixation on their internal world and develop without the influence of the external world.

Children who dissociate can be unconsciously inviting parental figures to be intrusive or neglectful. Therefore the way to parent such a child effectively, without taking these invitations to replicate their past experience, is to find a middle ground between being intrusive and being neglectful (Box 5.3).

Box 5.3 Relationship replication: dissociation
Birth family experience

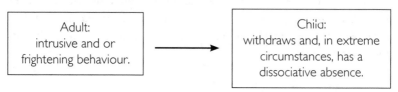

The parent is frightening or imposes unwanted intimacy when the child cannot physically escape. The child resorts to escaping in the only manner available to them by dissociating.

Foster/Adoptive family experience

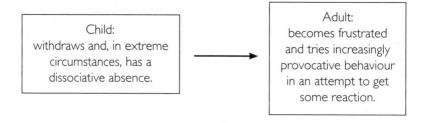

The child is keenly aware of the potential for danger and/or intrusion that they cannot escape from and so dissociates. The carer may read the behaviour as rudeness or inattention and so tries to 'wake' the child from their 'daydream' with increasingly intrusive attempts.

SUMMARY: The intrusive or frightening parenting has resulted in the child's need to withdraw. The child's withdrawal has unconsciously invited their carer to be frightening and/or intrusive. The carer has accepted the invitation.

Empathic behaviour management strategies: zoning out

Paradoxically, because dissociation is such a passive form of coping, as carers assist their children to abandon their need to 'zone out' the children may develop other, more active, ways of coping. These new ways are likely to be more behaviourally challenging methods of relating to their carers, for example, attachment-seeking, rage outbursts, controlling behaviour. It is important for carers to bear in mind, and reassure themselves, that these are, in fact, extremely encouraging signs of progress.

EBM for carers

RESPONSIVE EBM FOR CARERS

Once carers have taken the time thoroughly to prepare themselves for their own reactions to the dissociative outbursts, including reading this chapter, they are likely to find that their approach instinctively changes in light of the shift to the new ways of understanding their child's dissociations.

PREVENTATIVE EBM FOR CARERS

It is important, when parenting a child who zones out, that carers understand the cause of the child's difficulty and address it in the light of that understanding. It is equally important to understand, in advance, the potential 'emotional snags' (i.e. buttons that might be pressed) that carers may become aware of in their own personalities, when they experience the dissociative episodes of their children, and why these snags are triggered.

In the moment of a dissociative absence, therefore, it is important for carers to acknowledge and understand their own feelings about the episode so that they can respond empathically in the light of their rational understandings rather than their instinctive reactions. Carers can use the strategies in Chapter 2 to understand and address their own instinctive reactions.

Understanding the past

If carers do not have much information about their child's experiences, particularly those in the child's first three years, it is very important that carers try as hard as they can to get as much information as they can so that they can do their best to understand their child's need to dissociate and in order to help them through the difficulty.

When carers have collected as much information as they can about their child's past it is important to go through it and make a note of the things that their child would have found very stressful and/or frightening during their early experience. Carers can use the information to think about what types of experience their child would have attempted to avoid. This may include situations that were external to the child, for example, violence and being left alone for long periods, and situations that were internal to their child, for example hunger, sadness and rage. This understanding will help carers to identify what it is that their child is trying to escape when they zone out. Box 5.1 may be a helpful starting point to help carers to analyse what experience has caused their child's dissociation.

Having done this, it can be useful for carers to go back over the previous few weeks and try to understand what was going on around their child before they zoned out. Sometimes the triggers may be very subtle, sensory triggers, which can therefore be very hard to identify. If this is the case then the child is unlikely to be able to access the verbal information about why their dissociation has been triggered and so will not be able to explain it to their carer.

When carers feel that they have an understanding of the things that may cause their child to dissociate then they can use this understanding to inform their empathic commentary and give their child a potted idea of why they think the child's dissociations occur.

EBM for children

Responsive EBM for children

The key thing for carers to remember when their child has zoned out is that the goal is to find a middle ground between trying to intrusively 'wake them up' and leaving the child to it. This middle ground will enable carers to find a route into allowing their child to experience them as someone who can regulate the child's emotions without forcing them into an unwanted interaction. The carers' goal is not to yank their child back into consciousness but to make consciousness a warm and safe place for the child to return to when they feel able to.

Responsive empathic commentary

Empathic commentary is one of the most useful strategies to use when a child has zoned out. Empathic commentary for dissociative episodes will help carers to provide a compassionate understanding of what is going on inside their child's mind, but out loud so that their child also learns about their own inner world by using the carer's mind as an emotional mirror. The Golden Rules in Box 3.9 (Chapter 3) will help carers to devise their commentary for their child's dissociative episodes. Box 5.4 provides some examples of empathic commentary statements that carers can use whilst their child is zoned out.

Box 5.4 Responsive empathic commentary for dissociative episodes

The following are some examples of the empathic commentary statements that carers can use during dissociative episodes to help their children to manage their need to isolate themselves. These can be used as a starting point but carers should feel free to come up with their own.

- 'OK, I think you've needed to disappear for a bit. I wonder what it is that has made you need to do that.'
- 'Something about me asking you to do your homework has really stressed you out, hasn't it? You need to shut down for a little bit.'
- 'Ah, I think you're feeling very stressed about something. I think that you need to zone out sometimes when that happens because you had too much stress to cope with when you were little.'
- 'I wonder if it was hearing me tell Phillip off that has stressed you out and made you need to disappear into your head for a while. I understand, adults getting cross used to be so scary for you at home.'
- 'Bedtimes are so stressful for you, aren't they? They make you want to shut down and not think or talk to anyone. I'm so sorry that bedtimes used to be so scary for you.'
- 'When people ask you to do something and you really don't want to it really upsets you, so much so that it makes you zone out a bit to escape. I understand, we'll deal with it together when you can cope with it.'

Tentative contact

A good way for carers to provide their children with some middle ground between being entirely alone and being intruded upon is to offer very gentle, tentative contact. This can be done in a variety of ways. Touch can be effective but it can feel too powerful, bordering on intrusive, in some cases; however, there are other ways too. Zoned-out children may not be able to access visual stimuli so carers may need to get creative with providing the child with a path out of their own mind via their other senses (touch, sound, smell). Box 5.5 contains some ideas on how to use tentative contact when children have zoned out.

Box 5.5 Tentative contact

Here are a few examples of tentative contact that can help zoned-out children to understand that being interactive with their carer in times of stress is safe and possibly even useful. Carers might like to start with the most indirect forms of contact and move on to others if their child responds positively. Carers should not try to get a reaction from their child but just attempt to make the world outside the child's head feel safer and more approachable, so it is useful for carers to settle into the following activities and not feel the need to rush.

- *Make the child comfortable*: Carers should treat zoned-out children as if they are toddlers who have drifted off to sleep. Carers might like to cover the child in a blanket.
- *Attentive companionship*: Carers can sit by the side of their child whilst keeping themselves occupied with something else, for example, watching TV, reading, etc. but chatting quietly and calmly to their child. This will allow the child to hear their carer's voice and use it as an anchor back to reality if they can.
- *Reading aloud*: Carers could try reading quietly beside their child so that the child can hear the carer's voice for the reasons detailed above.
- *Singing*: Nursery rhymes or any calm tune that the carer and child like can be a way to bridge the gap between them when the child has zoned out.
- *Sensory transitional object*: It's best for carers to be present during a child's dissociation but if it is not possible then carers could leave something that their child will connect with them on a sensory level, e.g. a t-shirt that the carer wore the previous day.
- *Holding the child's hand*: Whilst carers do something else, for example, reading, watching TV, they can hold their child's hand or gently move the child's hand to be in contact with them in some way.
- *Rhythmical touch*: Carers could gently stroke their child's hand or arm whilst they sit next to the child. Or carers could try gently drumming their fingertips on the palm of the child's hand. Again, this is not to wake the child up but to make them feel safe while they have retreated into their own mind.

Positive reunion

When the child comes out of their absence, it's important that carers welcome them back as if they've woken up from a nap. This can be done with a big smile, showing the child how pleased the carer is to have them back and then the carer can commentate on where they think the child has been and why, for example, 'Oh there you are! (big smile) it's lovely to have you back! I think you got worried about those loud voices you heard so you had to disappear for a bit.'

PREVENTATIVE EBM FOR CHILDREN

Understanding the past with your child

When carers have used the 'understanding the past' exercise for themselves (above), and come up with some ideas about why their child might need to zone out at times, they could talk this through with them in a way that is honest but is sensitive to their emotional state and in a way that they can understand.

Empathic commentary (preventative)

Empathic commentary can be used by carers to pre-empt their child's need to zone out (Box 5.6). Carers should talk the child through what they think is going on internally for the child, that is, talk through what they think their child might be feeling or what they might start to feel if a dissociation trigger occurs. This, over time, is likely to help decrease the child's need to dissociate.

Box 5.6 Preventative empathic commentary for dissociative episodes

Here are some examples of the empathic commentary statements that carers can use during dissociative episodes to help their child to manage their need to isolate themselves.

- 'Oh my word! That was loud! You're getting really worried about Joe and Andy shouting and squealing aren't you? Loud noises sometimes meant that Mummy and Daddy were hurting each other and you weren't safe. I'm sorry you're worried.'
- 'I know you get really upset when you can't have chocolate every time you ask for it. I think it makes you worry that I'll let you go hungry and it's no wonder because you used to be hungry so often!'

- 'I like to come and tuck you into bed at night because I want you to know that you're safe and loved but I do understand that it sometimes makes you very frightened because of the way that Steve used to touch you at night times and you couldn't escape! I'm so sorry that that happened and that you still get scared but I want to keep you safe and help you to feel less scared.'

Whenever empathic commentary is used it is important that the Golden Rules (see Box 3.9, Chapter 3) are used.

Bursting the bubbles

During a calm time when there aren't any stresses around, it can be useful for carers to talk with their child about what it feels like when they zone out. This conversation can help carers to develop more empathy for their child's need to dissociate. In addition, carers' reflections on how the dissociations make sense for the child will help children to understand their own internal worlds more effectively.

Carers and the child should try to come up with a descriptive image and creative language for what the absences feel like, for example, for Misha her absences were like being in a bubble. The child can be encouraged to draw this image in the middle of a piece of paper. The following questions can then be used alongside the carer's understanding of the child's needs to dissociate to facilitate a conversation between carer and child about the dissociations. Carers should encourage their child to write and draw the answers and understandings around the central image.

- What does being in a bubble feel like?
- What is good about being in one of your bubbles?
  - Do they protect you from any bad things? If so, what are those things?
- What are the bad things about being in one of your bubbles?
  - Do you miss out on anything whilst you're in there?
- Can anyone else get inside the bubble with you?
- Would you like anyone to be in the bubble with you or is it best to be in there by yourself?
- When did you first go inside a bubble?
- Are there times when you've needed to go into a bubble more than others?
- What's the longest time that you've stayed out of a bubble?

Box 5.7 Things to remember about dissociative episodes

Understanding how it makes sense

- What might look like inattention, laziness and/or daydreaming may be dissociative absences.
- The potential that the absences are caused by a medical condition should be investigated by raising the issue with the child's doctor.
- Dissociative episodes, in the absence of medical explanation, are often caused by a child's unconscious strategy, learned in infancy, for avoiding otherwise inescapable danger, distress and/or pain.
- This strategy can be understood as 'passive coping'.
- Dissociation enables a child's brain to release neurochemicals that alleviate pain, numb emotions, promote immobility and inhibit the urge to cry out.

Understanding what to do

- EBM for carers:
  - Responsive strategies:
    - A good understanding for a carer of what their own emotional reactions are likely to be can help them to be calmer and less judgemental of their own reactions.
    - Carers should not try to deny or mask their feelings but understand them and work with them.
  - Preventative strategies:
    - Carers can benefit from developing an awareness of their own reactions to dissociative episodes.
    - Understanding the past.
- EBM for children:
  - Responsive strategies.
    - Responsive empathic commentary.
    - Tentative contact.
    - Positive reunion.
  - Preventative strategies:
    - Understanding the past.
    - Preventative empathic commentary.
    - Bursting bubbles.

CHAPTER 6 .

The High-Energy Child

Many developmentally traumatised children display difficulties with attention, hyperactivity and impulsivity. As explored in Chapter 1, this is very understandable when the experience-dependent nature of the development of the frontal lobes of the brain is taken into account. As well as being common effects of early abuse and neglect, difficulties with attention, hyperactivity and/or impulsivity also form the diagnostic criteria for attention deficit hyperactivity disorder (ADHD). This said, though many of the difficulties experienced by developmentally traumatised children can be classified in diagnostic terms, there is much philosophical and ontological debate amongst practitioners and researchers about which is the 'truer' way of defining such psychological difficulties.

For the purposes of day to day work with adopted and fostered children I tend to take quite a pragmatic point of view on this issue. If a child presents with attention, hyperactivity and impulsivity difficulties and there is evidence that they have experienced developmental trauma then it is useful to address the trauma in the first instance, as the root of the problem. There are, however, children for whom tailored parenting and even specialist therapeutic techniques are not enough. In these cases it can be beneficial, if an ADHD diagnosis is appropriate, for medication to be used to facilitate therapeutic work, including therapeutic parenting. Overall, however, therapeutic parenting for most developmentally traumatised children with high energy levels can be very effective without medication.

Examples

The following are examples of high-energy, developmentally traumatised children. I have aimed to include examples that demonstrate a range of difficulties with which high-energy children often present.

Elijah

Elijah was a four-year-old boy who was adopted when he was seven months old. The family's neighbours had raised the alarm, reporting that they frequently heard Elijah crying, relentlessly, for days at a time. In his short life, prior to being adopted, Elijah had largely been ignored by his birth mother, his father was not around and he was the only child in the home. Elijah's mother had tried hard with her son, when she could, but she suffered from severe depression and had very little support from her family or friends.

Claire and Peter, Elijah's adoptive parents, described that they had fallen in love with Elijah as soon as they met him. However, their description of Elijah became increasingly negative as they recounted how difficult he had become as he got older.

On the whole, Elijah appeared to be a carefree, happy boy but his parents found his high energy levels tough to deal with. Elijah's school reported that they had no concerns about him and said that he socialised and learned well.

It became clear that the family was under considerable stress; there were four children in the home and, in addition to the parents' concerns about Elijah, the couple were also concerned about the behaviour of their 15-year-old daughter. It appeared that the vast majority of the childcare responsibility was shouldered by Claire.

In one-to-one play observations it became apparent that Claire was comfortable and confident in allowing Elijah to lead the play; she followed him attentively and interacted with smiles and enthusiasm. As a result, Elijah focused on activities for quite some time and appeared settled and calm. Peter was just as enthusiastic as his partner had been in the play session with his son, but he led the play quite rigidly and became focused on particular activities that he enjoyed and that he wanted his son to enjoy with him. Consequently, the two played independently of one another and Elijah flitted from one activity to another, never seeming to be able to settle. In contrast to the play session with his mother Elijah became, at times, overexcited with his father, shouted to get his attention and, at one point, Elijah started to throw sand out of the sand pit.

Claire and Peter later described that Elijah's behaviour during the session with his father was typical of his behaviour at home.

Elijah's parents were convinced that their adopted son should be given a diagnosis of ADHD even after it was investigated and ruled out. Unfortunately their focus on the need for a diagnosis resulted in Elijah's parents struggling to make use of any therapeutic approach to understanding their son's context-dependent attention and hyperactivity problems.

Joshua

At the time that I knew Joshua he had been living with his short-term foster carer for the previous eight months. Joshua was a ten-year-old boy who, along with his two brothers, had been neglected by his parents, due to their drug addictions. The addictions meant that the family 'sofa-surfed' most of the time. This resulted in Joshua and his brothers experiencing a great deal of instability and being surrounded by adults who were not attuned to their needs. Joshua also witnessed his father being very violent towards his mother. In addition, when his mother was not under the influence of drugs or preoccupied with fear regarding the domestic violence, she seemed to be able to respond sensitively to her children.

Joshua had rage outbursts approximately twice a week both at school and at home, he was reported to be constantly full of energy and found it very difficult to concentrate. Potentially as a result of this, Joshua would frequently play the class clown at school and would get into lots of trouble for not being able to control his energy and for failing to complete his work.

Joshua struggled to engage meaningfully with therapeutic work, which aimed to address his past trauma. Indeed whenever difficult thoughts entered Joshua's mind he would behave quite chaotically and become very difficult to contain physically and emotionally. During the course of my work with Joshua he was diagnosed with ADHD by a paediatrician and started taking medication for it. Joshua reported feeling much happier as he was getting into considerably less trouble at school. He was also more able to make use of his carer's therapeutic parenting and meaningfully engage in therapeutic work with me. Joshua's carer and teachers had previously struggled to understand and empathise with his past experiences and how they related to his behaviour. However, they all became more compassionate and encouraging with Joshua after he started taking the ADHD medication.

Typical reward-punishment strategies for high-energy children

The behaviour of children who are always on the go is frequently seen as naughtiness. Excessive amounts of energy lead children (as they would with any of us) into behaving in a manner that causes other people problems. Box 6.1 gives a list of behaviours that are commonly seen in developmentally traumatised children with lots of energy.

Box 6.1 Examples of the behaviour of children with high energy levels

- Struggling to sit still to complete an activity.
- Difficulties in sticking with one activity for more than a few minutes.
- Play becoming overexcited and/or dangerous.
- Impulsive behaviour, e.g. running across a road to get a football regardless of the traffic.
- Fiddling.
- Unwillingness to stop and listen.
- Easily distracted.
- Struggling to wait for their turn.
- Poor sleep.

Each of the individual behaviours listed in Box 6.1 could be, and commonly are, dealt with using reward-punishment strategies, for example, forcing a child to sit in one place until their homework is finished, having their football taken away for running across the road or offering a star on a star chart if instructions are listened to and acted upon.

In the case of children who do not sleep well the most common strategies are reward-punishment based, for example 'controlled crying', whereby parents/carers limit the amount of reward, that is, attention, that a child will get from waking, and the crying, by limiting their interaction with them. Whilst controlled crying is most often thought of as being used with babies and younger children, the strategies used with older children are typically based on the same principles. Simply replace crying with, for example, a child's disruptive behaviour in their bedroom, that is, repeatedly calling out at night or persistently getting out of bed.

All of the difficulties mentioned above could be seen as attachment-seeking behaviours and, in developmentally traumatised children, we need to respond to that need as a priority.

These high-energy characteristics are very challenging to deal with and using reward-punishment thinking, with the developmentally traumatised children who display them, overwhelmingly leads to frustration and negativity in adult-child relationships.

Making sense of energetic children

The most influential aspects of the EBM model for high-energy children (Figure 6.1) are the need to relate, emotional regulation, hard-wired survival strategies and the effects of experience on brain and biology (in bold).

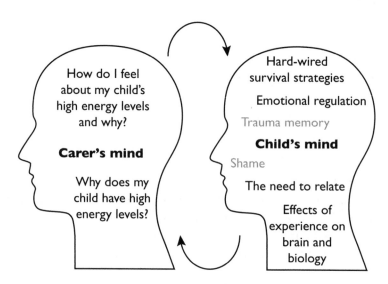

Figure 6.1 EBM model of children with high energy levels

The need to relate

Fundamental to understanding the need for high energy levels in many developmentally traumatised children is an acceptance that children are evolutionarily and neurologically driven by their need to relate to another person.

Broadly speaking there are two types of relational environment that might lead to a child developing a strategy of high energy levels. First, in the case of physical abuse by a carer, the infant learns that they must balance their simultaneous needs to relate to their caregiver and be vigilant that their caregiver might cause them harm. In other words, these children experience the constant stress of needing someone to be close to them but also needing to be wary of their closeness.

Second, high-energy behaviour is also an adaptive behaviour for a baby who has been neglected. Such children need to be consistently vigilant for rare opportunities for interaction with their carers. If a child in this environment had the full range of energy levels, that is, was relaxed and calm sometimes, then they would inevitably miss out on crucial opportunities to get their needs met. Children in neglectful environments learn that they will not get their needs met by their carers without making a great deal of effort.

Emotional regulation

In terms of the ability to regulate emotions, children who have consistently high energy levels have a limited range of emotional expression. These children are stuck between 7 and 10 on their emotional thermostat and they very rarely relax enough to go below this, even at night time. Consequently, developmentally traumatised, high-energy children often have poorer sleep for a shorter time than other children.

As a result of their early experience, the brains of high-energy children have adapted to make sure that the child can sustain the effective strategy, that is, remaining constantly vigilant and mobile, by ensuring that they are hard-wired and neurochemically programmed.

Hard-wired survival strategies

In order to understand how the particular behaviours of developmentally traumatised children make sense as survival strategies it is important to think carefully about the function of such behaviours, that is, what effect does the behaviour have? When ideas about this have been developed it is possible to look backwards, using the information gathered about the child's early experience, to speculate about how the behaviours might have been useful for their physical and emotional survival. The usefulness of these strategies does not imply that they are consciously employed; indeed, as they were developed in infancy, they are invariably unconscious strategies.

In the case of children with high energy levels, their behaviour often succeeds in bringing their carer closer to them in times of emotional stress (see Chapter 3). High-energy behaviour also has the potential to replicate behaviour in adults that the child is familiar with (see Box 6.2), which is familiar, predictable and thus has elements of perceived safety even if it is ultimately distressing.

Box 6.2 Relationship replication: high-energy children

Birth family experience

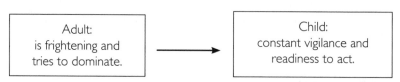

The parent is frightening and dominating. Child is biologically prepared for fight or flight and consequently constantly full of nervous energy and unable to concentrate on the trivialities of day to day life.

Foster/Adoptive family experience

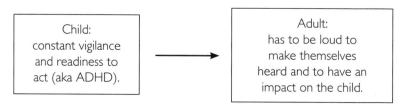

The child is biologically prepared to defend themselves and unable to concentrate on day to day activities. The carer asserts themselves in increasingly punitive ways in order to have an impact on the otherwise unreachable child.

SUMMARY: The dominating and/or frightening parenting has resulted in the child's vigilance. The child has unconsciously invited the carer to be frightening and/or dominating. The carer has accepted the invitation.

OR...

Birth family experience

The parent is psychologically, emotionally and/or physically unavailable to the child during their infancy and so the child develops strategies which ensure that they cannot be ignored and consequently are more likely to get their needs met.

Foster/Adoptive family experience

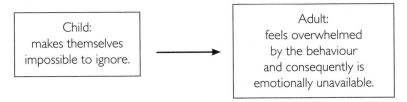

The child is biologically programmed by their parenting to be hard to ignore. The carer becomes overwhelmed by the child's high-energy behaviour and either ignores it or emotionally distances themselves from the child, consequently becoming emotionally unavailable.

SUMMARY: The neglectful parenting has resulted in the child becoming impossible to ignore. The child has unconsciously invited the carer to be unavailable. The carer has accepted the invitation.

Developmentally traumatised, high-energy children learn that their survival depends upon on consistently high energy levels (Box 6.4). If such a child were to take any opportunity to relax then they may be vulnerable either via direct physical threat or by not extracting the limited available resources from a neglectful carer.

Frustratingly for carers, and sadly for children, this high-energy strategy for survival is also active at night. Many high-energy children have a great deal of difficulty sleeping. Take a moment to think about what it must be like to live in constant fear and/or needing to be constantly vigilant. Add to this your frailty; if you do need to protect yourself or force someone to do what you need them to do for you,

you stand very little chance because you are so small and powerless. Then imagine what it would be like to try to abandon yourself to the paralysed vulnerability of sleep. For many developmentally traumatised children, having a long, solid, sound sleep has been proven to be a ridiculously foolhardy idea.

Box 6.3 Infant experiences that make sense of high energy levels

Prolonged exposure to any of the following can promote the need for adaptive survival strategies and consequently trigger atypical cortisol levels and thus lead to atypical brain development in infants:

- *Neglect*: Babies need the constant availability of a carer and high levels of energy and careful vigilance can be very helpful in attracting the care of a hard to reach parent.
- *Physical abuse*: Vigilance for danger, which requires constant high physiological arousal, is a very protective strategy in an environment of physical threat.
- *Rough handling*: e.g. over-enthusiastic play, insensitive, careless handling. Both high levels of alertness and an abundance of physical energy are very useful for babies who have to cope with lots of rough handling, i.e. to enable them to move away quickly, tense muscles to protect themselves or scream to deter an aggressive approach.
- *The anger/fear of others*: e.g. domestic abuse. People who are frightening and/or frightened tend to be unpredictable. A baby who is vigilant and has an abundance of energy is better equipped to react to unpredictable behaviour than a baby who is relaxed and calm.

All of the above applies to adult behaviour and that of other children. In environments where older children are not supervised appropriately their behaviour may evoke the need for high energy and vigilance in babies.

These adaptive survival strategies, developed in response to early abuse and/or neglect, are then backed up thanks to the way that babies' brains develop in response to their early environments.

Effects of experience on brain and biology

As discussed above, the adaptive, unconscious strategies developed in early infancy become hard-wired to ensure that children continue to use the most effective relational strategies for the environment into which they are born.

There is some evidence to suggest that the brain decides what is 'normal' for a baby in terms of their levels of cortisol (stress hormone) by the age of just six months (Lewis and Ramsay 1995). Therefore if a child has experienced consistently high quantities of cortisol prior to six months because of inhabiting a high stress environment then this level of cortisol will be taken as being the normal, appropriate level that the brain will use as a default level by which it can compare the stimulation/stress levels of any given situation.

Now imagine a child, whose normal levels of cortisol and emotional energy represents what most people would consider high levels, that is, from 7 to 10 on our emotional thermostat, being placed in an environment that has a full range, that is, 1 to 10. Consider how it must feel for that child to have to live with levels of arousal that are far below anything that they are biologically programmed to understand. In such a context the child is surrounded by, what is to them, a sub-zero arousal environment. In a typical home setting the child is, by and large, expected to occupy the lower end of the emotional thermostat. The child is then compelled, in order to give sense to this new world, to raise the level of energy in the environment in order that they can feel some degree of stimulation.

To help us to understand what this must feel like we would have to apply a sub-zero amount of arousal to our own environment. Try using the exercise in Box 6.4 below to understand what it is like for a high-energy child to live in a typical foster home and be expected to conform to their new carers' expectations about the appropriate levels of energy.

Consequences of using reward-punishment thinking with high-energy children

If a child has an abundance of energy, for example, due to being neurologically hard-wired for fear and safety-seeking behaviour, then any strategy that fails to address that underlying need is likely to result in an escalation of the problem as the child redoubles their efforts to apply their survival strategy.

If the high energy levels of a developmentally traumatised child are understood and addressed using reward-punishment thinking then they are likely to internalise in their own mind the implied feelings of the people that apply the strategies, that is, 'My emotions cannot be understood', 'My emotions (that I don't have control of) make me bad' and/or 'My emotions deserve to be punished'.

Using reward-punishment strategies in these situations is, in effect, punishing the child for the survival strategy that has kept them safe and the resultant neurological drives. This makes as much sense as punishing a child for eating, or breathing, that is, it is detrimental to the child and extremely unlikely ever to be effective.

Empathic behaviour management strategies for high-energy children
EBM for carers
RESPONSIVE EBM FOR CARERS

It is useful for carers to use the understandings that they have built up of their own 'emotional snags', that is, those emotional reactions that derive from their own experience and can be triggered by their child, regarding high energy/poor concentration behaviour. Taking the time to build up these understandings will impact on carers' instinctive responses to the high-energy behaviour of their child when it occurs.

It is important for carers to try to remain empathic and to understand the high-energy behaviour of their child as attempts to communicate unconsciously about their past trauma and thus their parenting needs.

PREVENTATIVE EBM FOR CARERS

In order to help carers to understand what it might feel like to be a high-energy child they can use the self-reflection and empathy building exercises in Chapter 2. It may also be useful to try the exercise in Box 6.4.

Box 6.4 What it feels like to be a high-energy child in a low-energy environment

Imagine that you have been kidnapped. You are taken from your home and your typical life and put in a dark room; you cannot see or hear anything.

What is your first reaction? What do you do?

One week later and you are still locked in your dark, silent room. You are provided with food and water but this arrives via a hole in the door. You never get to speak to anyone or even hear a voice.

How do you feel?

What do you do?

Thinking about the levels of sensory deprivation that we might experience in such a situation helps us to understand what it is like for a high-energy child living within an environment with much lower levels of energy and stimulation than is 'normal' for them. Many of the feelings and strategies that you will have identified in the questions above will be similar to the feelings and strategies that high-energy children will experience in a comparatively lower-energy home.

It is essential for carers thoroughly to prepare their understanding of their own emotional responses to high-energy behaviour *prior* to any attempt to deal directly with their child. This understanding will help to increase the levels of empathy that carers feel for the child's need for high energy levels.

EBM for children
RESPONSIVE EBM FOR CHILDREN
Rhythmical calming
Rhythmical calming was introduced in Chapter 4, when methods of soothing children through rage outbursts were explored. The techniques listed in Box 6.5 are examples of rhythmical calming that can be particularly successful for high-energy children.

Box 6.5 Rhythmical calming for high-energy children
The following are examples of rhythmical calming that carers might like to try when their child is particularly high in energy. During calmer times these can also be used as preventative strategies to enable high-energy children to

develop some regulation of their emotions and therefore their energy levels. All of the following strategies should be done in partnership between carer and child; carers are a crucial element in calming their high-energy children.

- Rolling a ball back and forth between carer and child.
- Hand-clapping games, perhaps with singing too.
- Singing nursery rhymes.
- Marching.
- Trampolining.
- Dancing together.
- Playing drums together.
- Swing ball.
- Kicking a ball against a wall.
- Rocking in a rocking chair (either with the carer sitting beside the child or with the child sitting on the carer's knee).
- Gently swinging the child in a blanket (and yes, with enough assistance, I have done this, whilst singing nursery rhymes, with 15-year-olds).
- Blowing bubbles.

Children will often find their own ways to calm themselves rhythmically. This is, in fact, what a high-energy child is doing when they persistently run up and down the hallway or insist upon kicking a football against the back door. Therefore, if it is possible, carers should allow their child to continue with their intuitive rhythmical calming, but join them in it.

In cases when allowing the child to continue would be dangerous or too disruptive, carers should adapt the instinctive soothing behaviour rather than introduce a completely new activity; it's obviously appealing to the child and possibly effective as it is. For example, if someone is likely to get knocked over in the hallway, it may be possible to divert the child to do their running in the garden and for the carer to do it with them. The ball kicking could be transplanted to the back wall of the house rather than against the back door. Such redirections should be done with empathy rather than reprimand, as reprimand might elevate the child's, already activated, expectation of conflict and need for high levels of energy.

Many children instinctively calm themselves via putting things in their mouths; this is potentially another example of intuitive rhythmical calming. Joshua (discussed earlier in this chapter) used to like chewing bits of paper, any paper he could get his hands on. His carers, understandably, tried to discourage this behaviour and any time they saw him chewing they would ask him what he had in his mouth and if it was paper they would tell him to spit it out and not to do it again. This led Joshua to lie to his carers about what he was doing and conceal his paper chewing. One possible alternative, if carers really couldn't get their heads around allowing him to chew paper, would have been to encourage Joshua to chew chewing gum (as much as many carers dislike children having chewing gum, in this case it has potential as a valuable therapeutic tool). This would have allowed Joshua to soothe himself in a way that he knew was reliable and effective whilst being more socially appropriate.

Attachment time

This technique is included in Chapter 3 in relation to attachment-seeking children; however, it is equally useful for children who struggle to sit down or stick with one activity. As explored earlier in the chapter, Elijah's wandering concentration was due to a lack of emotional containment and the absence of an available adult mind. The attachment time strategy allows a high-energy child to borrow the frontal lobes of an available adult to help sustain their interest in, and fascination with, a task.

There are a few alterations that carers should make to the attachment time instructions in Chapter 3, in order to use attachment time with high-energy children (Box 6.6), but it is useful to refer back to these as a starting point.

Box 6.6 Attachment time adaptations for high-energy children

Refer to the original attachment time activity in Chapter 3, but in order to use it with high-energy children the following adaptations can be useful.

- Carers should limit the amount of activities that are included on the attachment time menu. Having five activities on the menu and two available for any one session is likely to be a good starting point. Carers may feel that they are able to add in more as time goes on and they start to feel that their child can concentrate for longer.

- The length of attachment time sessions should be shortened: 20 minutes may be a good starting point. It may be possible to extend the time if the child responds well.

- Carers should take their time when introducing increases in time and number of activities. It is important to ensure that there is at least a week of solid engagement and concentration with attachment time before making any changes.

- It is crucial for carers to show very focused interest in their child's experience of the activity and for them to commentate (using Box 3.9 Empathic commentary: golden rules) intensely.

- A room with very few distractions should be used.

- Carers will need to avoid taking the invitation to discipline or reprimand their child for wanting to move on to the next activity. Instead carers should move with them and continue to attend to the child's subjective experience of the activity.

- In the beginning children are likely to want to move between activities very quickly. However, the devoted attention and help of their carer will regulate the child's excitement and/or energy. After using this strategy for a quite some time the child should be able to stick with one activity for longer.

Sleep soothing

Many developmentally traumatised, high-energy children have trouble getting to sleep, will wake in the night and rise surprisingly early. They seem, in many cases, not to need as much sleep as other children.

Due to the high-energy child's survival strategy of neurochemically reinforced continual vigilance (as discussed earlier in the chapter), they may not be able to sleep for as long as other children and appear to be just as refreshed by smaller amounts of sleep. In the short term it is useful for carers to adjust their mind-set about this rather than persisting with ever more extreme strategies for persuading such a child to sleep for nine or ten hours a day.

Sleep has often been a very vulnerable state for developmentally traumatised children and so the sensible thing, from a survival point of view, has been to limit the amount of sleep. Consequently, in order to tackle a developmentally traumatised, high-energy child's sleep difficulties we must deal not with their need for sleep but with their very real need to be awake.

When a developmentally traumatised child has trouble sleeping it is important, in the first instance, to deal with their need to feel safe. Carers should, therefore, treat the time that their child is awake, when they should be asleep, as an opportunity for attachment-building, much as they would with a young baby. Carers can encourage their child to stay in their own bed but do so with an understanding of the difficulties that they will have in separating from their carer. Box 6.7 provides some examples of sleep soothing strategies.

Box 6.7 Soothing poor sleepers

Key points

- Carer should get into the mind-set of seeing their child as a restless baby.
- It is useful for carers first to make sure that it is not the room itself that is distressing their child, then go with them into their room and work on making their room and bed a safe, restful place for them.
- Carers should match their child's energy levels, and gradually calm with them, rather than impose what level of energy they think the child should have.

Examples of strategies to try

- Carers can try providing their child with some form of physical contact. The best way is for carers to cosy up beside their child in or on their bed (if this breaches a Safe Care Policy then this should be discussed with carers' supervising social workers in advance).
- For some children cosying up together will be too intrusive initially so carers could try to hold their hand or stroke their arm whilst sitting on the floor beside them.
- When carer and child are cosy together carers can read their child a story or sing them nursery rhymes (even with teenagers, just be brave!).
- Carers can stroke their child's hair and talk soothingly about anything; the child's day, the carer's day, what's happening tomorrow, a TV programme they watched together.
- The rhythmical calming strategies may also be useful but they should be tailored for bedtime.
- If the child is too energetic to do any of these more sedate, soothing activities carers will have to respond with the more wakeful, rhythmical calming, strategies (Box 6.5).

Foster carers may need to speak with their supervising social worker about their organisation's Safe Care Policy when employing these sleep soothing strategies. It is crucial, however, to provide nocturnally restless, developmentally traumatised children with a positive, soothing experience and so it is important to find a way, in collaboration with the appropriate professionals, if necessary, to implement the soothing strategies.

When sleep soothing strategies have been applied for some time, and if it becomes apparent that the high-energy child is sleeping for longer periods, then it may be possible to start to employ some of the more typical techniques for helping them to settle without adult soothing.

PREVENTATIVE EBM FOR CHILDREN

Rhythmical scales

This strategy is called *rhythmical scales* because it uses a rhythmical calming strategy but it is practised like a musical scale. The rhythmical activity is used to travel up and down the child's energy levels. This enables the child to experience, using our thermostat metaphor, the full 1 to 10 range of their energy levels rather than their limited range. This also enables high-energy children to practise moving from one state to another so that, over time, they can internalise the experience and apply this emotional and energy regulation in day to day life.

It can be very effective to incorporate rhythmical scales into a story as this can help to capture children's attention and structure their energy levels. Box 6.8 contains a few examples of how rhythmical scales can be used.

Box 6.8 Rhythmical scales

Any of the following stories or other individualised ones can be used to help high-energy children to experience a broader range of energy levels and practise what it feels like to be in control of the movement between levels. It's important that carers do these exercises with their child and move up and down the scales with them.

Guard Duty

For this story use both of your real names where I have used Manjit and Parveen.

'Private Manjit and Private Parveen were two soldiers out marching (let's march like in the story). They were marching around the barracks on their way to guard the front gate. They had plenty of time and they were going at a normal pace.

On their way to the gate they marched past Sergeant Bob, who was sleeping in the sun. If they woke him up they'd be in trouble so they crept past him really slowly and carefully on tiptoes (let's creep past like in the story).

When Private Manjit and Private Parveen got past Sergeant Bob they had to hurry a bit because they were late, so they marched as fast as they possibly could (let's do that too, faster, faster we need to get there as quickly as we can! As fast as you can possibly go! But make sure you're still marching!).

Having been marching really quickly for a while, Manjit and Parveen could eventually see the front gate in the distance. Luckily, by this point, they had made up a little bit of time so they slowed right down and marched really slowly to get their breath back (let's march really slowly now).

After they'd gone really slowly for a while they saw the sergeant major in charge of the gate, come into view. They didn't want to look like they were slacking off so they sped up, but just a little bit, to their normal marching pace (march a bit quicker but not too quickly!). Until they finally arrived at the gate to guard it right on time!'

The Rough Sea

For this story you'll need a blanket and one of your child's favourite toys, a character toy, such as a doll or a teddy bear.

Ask your child to hold one end of the blanket with their arms wide apart and you do the same at the other end and put the toy in the middle of the blanket. Then you can start to tell the story.

'One day teddy was in his boat on the sea. It was lovely and calm for teddy on his boat; the sun was shining and the waves rocked him very gently (let's make teddy's boat rock really gently). But after a little while it started to get windier out at sea and the waves got a bit bigger and rougher (let's make the sea a bit rougher for teddy in his boat, only a bit rougher though). The wind got stronger and stronger and the waves got bigger and rougher (gradually ramp up the waves and encourage your child to do the same). Oh wow! It's really rough now! Hold on teddy! After a while the wind dropped just a little bit and teddy's boat moved around a little less, but it's still quite rough out at sea. But the wind is dropping even more, phew teddy, that's getting better but it's still a little bit windy. At long last the wind went away and teddy was back to rocking very gently on the waves.'

You can go up and down the levels of wind in this story as many times as it is enjoyable for you both.

Pillow Punch

You could also use this, much simpler, version of rhythmical scales and encourage your child to thump or slap a big cushion that you can hold between the two of you. Make sure it's a nice big cushion and that you will both be safe.

Then encourage your child to start hitting the cushion very gently and move them up to hitting harder and harder moving gradually through the energy levels. Make sure you encourage your child and join in with the level of energy with your voice and body language.

PREVENTATIVE EMPATHIC COMMENTARY

Empathic commentary can be used as a preventative and a responsive strategy for children who have lots of energy. Box 6.9 contains examples of empathic commentary statements that carers can try. It's very important whenever empathic commentary is used that the child's apparent mood and level of energy are mirrored in what is communicated verbally and non-verbally.

Box 6.9 Empathic commentary for high-energy children

The following are examples of empathic commentary statements for carers to try with high-energy children. Carers should feel free to make up their own but this should be done with reference to the Golden Rules in Box 3.9, Chapter 3.

- 'Wow! You're so full of beans! I wonder if you're getting ready to protect yourself like you used to have to!'
- 'Oh my word you've got so much energy and I can't keep up. I end up getting frustrated with you! Don't I? I'm sorry.'
- 'Oh it's so hard to concentrate on one thing at a time, you've never had any practice of anyone sitting and enjoying your play with you; no wonder it's hard to stay with one thing!'
- 'It's really hard for you to sit still today; you're so excited about everything!'

Box 6.10 Things to remember about high-energy children

Understanding how it makes sense

- High levels of energy can be adaptive in environments where there are high levels of danger and/or a child needs to make sure that they make the most of the limited availability of their parent/carer.

- High levels of energy, in developmentally traumatised children, can be viewed as sensible hypervigilance.
- Children without early experience of having their emotions and stresses understood and empathised with will struggle to regulate their emotions and energy levels in later childhood and adulthood.
- Developmentally traumatised, high-energy children often have limited access to the full range of emotional energy, i.e. on their emotional thermostat they are stuck between 7 and 10.
- The need for hypervigilance in infancy can become neurologically hard-wired. Consequently, environments in which there is anything less than very high energy levels can be the equivalent of sensory deprivation for these children. To avoid this apparent lack of stimulation, high-energy children will create higher energy levels in themselves and others by any means necessary.

Understanding what to do

- EBM for carers:
  - Responsive strategies:
    - A good understanding for a carer of what their own emotional reactions are likely to be can help them to be calmer and less judgemental of their own reactions.
    - Carers should not try to deny or mask their feelings but understand them and work with them.
  - Preventative strategies:
    - Carers can use the exercise in Box 6.4 to help them to understand what it is like for a high-energy child to live in a lower energy environment.
    - Carer should work on developing an awareness of their reactions to high-energy children.
    - Thoroughly researching a child's past will help carers to understand and value the high-energy strategies that children use.
- EBM for children:
  - Responsive strategies:
    - Rhythmical calming.
    - Attachment time (with adaptations).
    - Sleep soothing.
  - Preventative strategies:
    - Rhythmical scales.
    - Empathic commentary.

CHAPTER 7

Wrestling for Control

Controlling behaviour is an extremely common challenge of looking after children who have been traumatised by abuse and neglect. Its universality is all the more remarkable as it results from such a vast range of childhood experiences.

Feeling controlled by a child typically leads carers to feel that they need to escalate their control of the child, imagining that the child simply hasn't been parented with consistent enough 'rules and boundaries'. Acknowledging the subjective experience of feeling controlled by a child is important in identifying the reason why a child has developed this way of 'doing relationships'. Rather than acknowledge and understand the experience of feeling controlled it is far more enticing to identify the specific issues that are experienced day to day, for example, reliance on prescribed routines, not being amenable to boundaries, fussy eating, difficulty with sharing a carer, etc., and apply reward-punishment techniques to attempt to put a stop to the individual issues.

The difficulty of summarising control as an overarching issue in children who have been traumatised by abuse and/or neglect often leads to a failure to understand its importance. However, the influence it has, particularly on the relationships between children and their carers, can be enormous. Carers who look after controlling children can often feel dominated and/or manipulated, feelings which can be very damaging to intimate relationships.

Examples of controlling behaviour

In this section I will discuss two young people, Ricky and Misha, both of whom offer very extreme examples of contrasting types of controlling behaviour. Ricky actively controlled those around him whereas Misha was much more passive but equally controlling of her environment and her interactions with others. Most children who need to control will not be as extreme as either of these young people but the themes in their stories may be recognisable.

Ricky

Ricky was a 17-year-old boy who had lived with his mother and, intermittently, his father prior to being taken into the care of the local authority aged 11. He had been through 18 placement moves in the intervening six years. At the time that I met Ricky he was in a residential home.

Ricky's family experience was of brutal violence from his father towards him and his mother, and neglect on the part of his mother, who was perpetually preoccupied by terror and depression. Ricky had tried his best to look after his mother both emotionally and physically but he had, inevitably, failed as the task was too huge and his father too ferocious. Whilst Ricky had been in care all of the people who were important to him had died, his mother and father from suspected drugs overdoses and his grandmother from natural causes.

Ricky attempted to control everything in his life and if anyone tried to challenge his control, often in order to look after him effectively, he ignored them, called them names, mocked them, spat at them and/or assaulted them. Ricky was generally a very intimidating character. He would not respond to any attempt from the staff to limit his behaviour or in any way impact on his life, for example, Ricky dictated what time he went to sleep (he would stay up until 5am) and where he went (he would often be gone all day and no one would know where he was). In addition, Ricky would often be deliberately provocative with staff members to get a reaction from them and when they reacted he would be aggressive towards them.

Ricky would control any conversation he was party to, often not allowing anyone else to speak and at other times correcting, intimidating and mocking those talking to him. Ricky would also exert control by telling very plausible lies to wrong-foot people and create a situation in which he was the only one in possession of the truth. He would also tell fantastical lies that portrayed him as powerful, dangerous and important, in order to control people's perception of him. I'll discuss some of Ricky's lies in more detail in Chapter 8.

The staff at Ricky's residential home responded in different ways; many had tried to assert themselves in the face of his intimidation and became more intimidating than he was, consequently Ricky was often physically restrained. Other members of staff ignored Ricky as much as they possibly could, letting him do whatever he wanted to do, and they spoke about him with thinly veiled contempt and disgust. It is evident that the responses of staff members mirror those of Ricky's parents (see Box 7.1).

Overall, Ricky's need for control was absolute and his methods devastatingly effective.

Box 7.1 Relationship replication: control
Birth family experience

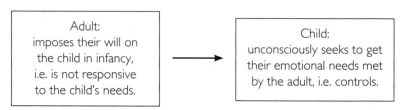

The parent is not responsive to the child's needs in infancy, that is, imposes their own emotional agenda on the child; this may take the form of neglect or intrusive care. The parent is therefore unable to regulate the emotions of the child, thereby creating a chaotic, frightening emotional environment. The child is fearful and protests in order to get their needs met and overcome the unpredictability of their experience. Consequently the child attempts, unconsciously, to control their environments.

Foster/Adoptive family experience

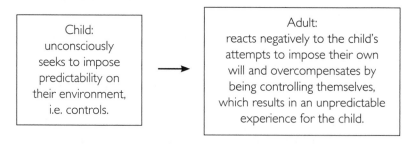

The child applies their unconscious strategy of imposing order on an emotionally, and possibly physically, chaotic world, generated via neglect or abuse. The carer reacts to the controlling of the child with stronger efforts to control in order to parent the child. This parenting necessitates the child having less power and control than the carer. The carer thus imposes their model of parenting upon the child, which makes the child feel less in control and therefore less safe.

SUMMARY: The misattuned and unresponsive parenting causes the child to create stability by controlling their environment. In their new home the child has unconsciously invited the carer to be controlling. The carer has accepted the invitation.

Misha

I have talked about Misha in Chapter 5 in relation to her dissociative absences. Misha's absences were a method of controlling her world and were just as powerful as Ricky's methods but in a very different way.

Misha was a 14-year-old girl who had lived with her long-term foster carers for two years. She was severely neglected when she lived with her mother, during which time she was frequently left locked, alone, in a bathroom for days at a time. Her mother suffered from severe mental health problems and interacted with Misha very little, even when Misha was not locked away. Misha had come into foster care aged 11 having missed out on approximately two years of school.

Misha would control by limiting her interaction with her environment and anyone in it. When Misha was asked to do anything she would either ignore the person asking and carry on with what she was doing, or completely freeze and absent herself from any interaction. In this way, Misha's control of her world was absolute; she rarely participated in, or even acknowledged, anything that she did not initiate.

Misha's dissociations created a high degree of frustration and anger in the adults around her and resulted, after some time, in her being frequently ignored and dismissed.

Other examples

As I have stated, Ricky and Misha displayed quite extreme levels of controlling behaviour. There are many more subtle ways in which children control their worlds and limit the extent to which others can have control over them.

Controlling behaviour can often take place with other children as well as caregivers. Many of the sibling conflicts that developmentally traumatised children get into are triggered by difficulties in sharing, deciding who's in charge or ideas about fairness. Though there are often complexities in the sibling relationships of developmentally traumatised children (see Chapter 10) these factors can, in part, be understood as arising from a feeling of having control taken away. I will discuss, later in this chapter, why not having control, an uncomfortable feeling that all of us have to tolerate at some point or another, is particularly threatening for developmentally traumatised children.

As discussed in Chapter 4, rage outbursts can often be triggered by limit setting and the word 'no', which, though entirely usual methods of parenting, are small ways in which adults exert control over their children. Whilst most children can tolerate these strategies, for many developmentally traumatised children allowing someone to have control over them has been proven in the past to be a costly mistake.

Typical strategies

As demonstrated in the stories of Ricky and Misha, above, the instinctive responses to the controlling behaviour of developmentally traumatised children are, most often, either to escalate and control in return, or to ignore and dismiss.

The instinct of most people, whose self-concept is strong enough to want to assert themselves, is to find a method of freeing themselves from the apparent manipulation and domination of the controlling child. The reward-punishment narrative of parenting supports this instinct and encourages carers to wrestle control away from their child and put themselves back in the driving seat.

Carers facing controlling behaviour will frequently apply the 'if you give them an inch they'll take a mile' principle, that is, they will accept the invitation to clamp down on all types of control that a child strives for, and offer ever decreasing autonomy. For example, when a child has been given the choice of what to have for their dinner, and the child then tries to dictate what they eat at every meal, perhaps becoming very angry when they can't and also wanting to control what others in the family eat too, the typical reward-punishment strategy would be to withdraw all choice from the child and have more structured set meals.

The alternative approach that carers are invited to take is to go to the opposite end of the spectrum and relinquish all power and agency in the relationship with their child, thus leaving the child with all the control they want and thus all of the responsibility too, for example, allowing a child to watch TV in bed until the early hours or allowing them to leave dirty crockery in their bedroom.

Making sense of the need for control

In attempting to understand the need of many developmentally traumatised children to sustain control over their environments, including the people around them, all of the elements of the EBM model (Figure 7.1) need to be considered: the need to relate, emotional regulation, trauma memory, hard-wired survival strategies, the effects of experience on brain and biology, and shame.

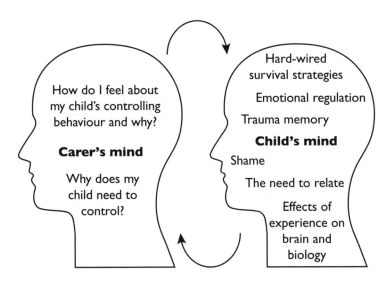

Figure 7.1 EBM model of children who need to control

The need to relate and emotional regulation

The fact that a developmentally traumatised child feels the compulsion to control can reveal a great deal about what the child's early experience of relating to others must have been like.

Babies are, initially, entirely unable to regulate their own emotions. In order to develop this regulation skill they need to relate to an adult and have the experience of an adult regulating their emotions for them. Therefore the absolute dependence of a baby on other people requires them to express their need without any reservation. This expression is an innate impulse; babies are not capable of 'reservation' at this stage and their expression of need is unconscious. The effect is that babies and toddlers are, of necessity, uncompromisingly controlling (you might want to try the baby cry exercise, Box 3.2 in Chapter 3, in order to experience this).

In order to move away from the infantile necessity for control, humans have to develop, through experience, trust in other people and the world around them. When that trust has been developed it is possible to tolerate other people having control because it is reasonable to believe that (1) we will get our turn and (2) others won't abuse their control over us.

Consequently it is reasonable to deduce that a child has developed control as a strategy because, in the past, relating to their primary carer in a reciprocal way has not regulated their emotions, has been dangerous or, in some other way, hugely aversive. Ultimately, babies are so physically and intellectually powerless that, in times of stress, they must amplify any method of control that they do have access to. Consequently, developmentally traumatised children cling on to their strategy of controlling their interactions with the world and the people within it.

In short, controlling children are likely to have experienced, in infancy, that the world (understood through interactions with their parent/carer) will not accommodate their needs without the child forcing it to do so. Therefore, in the absence of sensitive, attuned care, the child continues to need to force the world to indulge their infantile, emotional impulses. Unfortunately, later experiences of good care, which contradict this understanding of the world, will take far longer to have an impact because the early understanding has become hard-wired.

Trauma memory

For many developmentally traumatised children, early experiences of other people having control over them will have been anxiety provoking, dangerous and/or downright terrifying. Infant memories of such experiences in infancy are not stored in ways that hang together as rational, verbal stories but instead as emotionally charged clouds of sensation. Therefore controlling behaviour is likely to be sparked when one of these intangible clouds is triggered by some other sensory and/or emotional experience. The experience of feeling out of control in combination with raised levels of stress may well trigger attempts to control.

Hard-wired survival strategies and the effects of experience on brain and biology

In the case of controlling children, attempts to wrestle control from adults, or other children, may or may not have had any meaningful success in buffering the impact of their abusive and/or neglectful external world. However, there is, invariably, safety in the illusion of control that this offers children.

The need to control, when triggered frequently, will cause the infant brain to develop around this demand in order to support its use. It will, therefore, become hard-wired to ensure that the child has immediate and instinctive access to this strategy as the default option.

Shame

Babies are, initially, entirely egocentric, that is, they have no concept of the minds of others; to them, their experience is the only experience that exists. As I have already explored, early trauma often results in children remaining stuck in certain infantile stages of cognitive development. Consequently many developmentally traumatised children remain in that state, that is, accepting that they are the only ones who have control in the world.

The corollary of control is the feeling of responsibility. Therefore if children perceive that they should have control then they will understand what happens to them through the lens of sole, personal responsibility (Figure 7.2). I'm sure that many carers will recognise the difficulty that children often have in attributing any responsibility for their early experience to their parents. Indeed many children will take responsibility, themselves, for their abusive and/or neglectful treatment at the hands of their parents.

It follows therefore that if developmentally traumatised children have to be in control and view themselves as responsible as a result, then it is no surprise that they will blame themselves. This self-blame can also be viewed as shame.

This cycle is true of many developmentally traumatised children because they have an egocentric view of the world, that is, they have not developed the concept that there is anything beyond their internal experience.

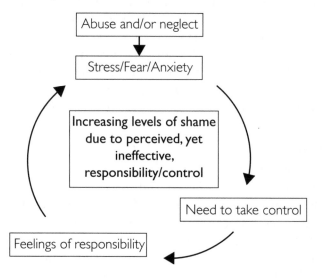

Figure 7.2 The control–responsibility cycle of traumatised children

Consequences of using reward-punishment thinking with children who control

In general, competing for control with a developmentally traumatised child who needs to control will simply result in the child redoubling their efforts to keep control themselves. Consequently, reward-punishment-based strategies will not be effective in reducing the controlling behaviour of traumatised children. Indeed, the effect of this strategy on the relationship with carers and developmentally traumatised children is likely to be an increase in anger, resentment and hostility, and a decrease in compassion and empathy.

Alternatively if carers allow their child to have complete control they will continue to feel completely responsible and not develop an ability to trust others. However, this strategy may make the child feel more comfortable in the short term.

Punishment of controlling behaviour, via reprimand, disapproval, etc., will invariably lead to an increase in a child's level of shame as they are unable to change their hard-wired survival strategy so easily but still feel responsible for changing it.

The use of reward-punishment strategies that don't directly address a developmentally traumatised child's need for control can have long-term negative outcomes for their emotional well-being and mental health (see Box 7.2).

Box 7.2 Potential consequences of not responding empathically to children who control

- Peer relationship difficulties.
- Lack of trust in relationships.
- Potential to be controlling in future relationships, e.g. domestic abuse.
- Eating disorders.
- Social isolation.
- Violent behaviour.
- Drug/alcohol abuse.
- Self-harm.

Empathic behaviour management strategies for children who control
EBM for carers
RESPONSIVE EBM FOR CARERS
When faced with a child's controlling behaviour the initial goal for carers is to notice when they are being invited to wrestle for control. It can be useful to hold in mind that the end goal in this situation is to dance with the child rather than wrestle with them.

The Tug of War Alarm
One playful way to deal with the invitations to wrestle for control with a child is to work together to sound the Tug of War Alarm.

If caring for a child feels to a carer like a tug of war then this may be a useful analogy to understand the difficulty and get carer and child working together. In a tug of war the harder one person pulls, the harder the other needs to pull in order not to lose ground. The reciprocal action perpetuates the behaviour of both people involved.

It is important for carers to notice when they are tempted to participate in the tug of war. Metaphorically speaking, if carers notice the existence of the rope then they will have a better chance of being able to agree to putting it down, so neither carer nor child have to pull. Carers can start by commenting on the process with their child when they notice that it is happening, for example, 'Oh look, we seem to be battling and it's not getting us anywhere!'

In time carers can also encourage their child to notice when the two of them are in a tug of war. It can then be made into a game, whereby either carer or child can sound the Tug of War Alarm. This can be done metaphorically, by someone simply saying out loud that this is what is going on, or the game can be made more playful by using a bell or a drum to sound the alarm. Whenever the alarm is sounded carer and child have to agree to put the rope down, come back to the issue later and find a different way to resolve it.

PREVENTATIVE EBM FOR CARERS

It is important that carers do some thorough preparation, and understand their own reactions, thoughts and feelings about their child's controlling behaviour, before they try to use the EBM strategies below directly with their child. The first two chapters of this book will also help with this process.

EBM for children
RESPONSIVE EBM FOR CHILDREN
Responsive empathic commentary
Whenever empathic commentary is used to try to regulate the emotions of a child, and to help them to understand their own internal worlds, the Golden Rules should be referred to (Box 3.9, Chapter 3). Box 7.3 offers some examples of empathic commentary statements for use when carers are faced directly with the controlling behaviour of their child.

Box 7.3 Empathic commentary for controlling behaviour

The following are examples of empathic commentary statements. They can be used as a starting point but carers should feel free to devise their own following the Golden Rules in Box 3.9, Chapter 3.

- 'Oh, it feels so much better when you get to make the decisions for yourself. I can understand that.'
- 'No wonder you want to take charge! Back when you were at home, you had to be, to keep you and your brother safe!'
- 'I'm so sorry that me making decisions for you feels so horrible. I think it's because grown-ups didn't make kind decisions for you in the past but we are going to have to stick with what I've said, I'm sorry.'
- 'Oh gosh, I made you feel so bad when I asked you to turn the TV off because you wanted to have control. I guess it must feel like I'm just being mean but I promise it's because I care about you.'
- 'It's no wonder that you want to tell your sister what to do! If you're not in control then you feel really bad! That makes sense. You've had to be in control of her for such a long time.'
- 'I'm so sorry that I can't quite understand yet why it feels so bad when you're not in control but I'm really going to try to work it out and try to make it feel better.'

PREVENTATIVE EBM FOR CHILDREN

Allowing control

The aim of *allowing control* is for carers to actively give children control of as many things as they can whilst not allowing them to take responsibility for things that would be unfair and/or inappropriate. In the allowing control technique carers are also communicating to their child that they understand that their need for control has meant that they have had to take a great deal of responsibility too. Carers should share in the enjoyment of their child when the child successfully manages both of these challenges.

Key points to remember when using the allowing control technique:

- Carers should make a big fuss about how well their child deals with the control and responsibility. Think of this as empathically sharing in their joy and success rather than praising them (praise derives from reward-punishment thinking and requires evaluation of the child).

- Carer and child should work together to actively facilitate the child's safe control.

- It is useful for carers to work out what the details of the allowing control task (see Box 7.4) will be before they give the control over to their child. Set them up to succeed.

- Carers should ensure that their child understands the details of what the task entails and give them the best chance of feeling good about being in control.

- It is important for carers to resist the temptation to take control back if the child struggles to manage the task that they have taken control of.

Box 7.4 Allowing control tasks

The following are examples of tasks that carers can use to cede control to their child. The examples can be used to help carers to generate ideas about the specific tasks that will give their child the best chance of feeling safely in control, succeeding and feeling good about themselves.

- Choose family activities:
  - Devise a schedule, e.g. for half-term week. The whole family can be involved but the child(ren) could be in charge of co-ordinating the schedule.
- Food:
  - Choosing which food to buy and writing a shopping list.
  - Shopping.
  - Choosing what to cook on a particular day.
  - Cooking.
  - Being in charge of setting a timer to say when the food will be ready and alerting you to the fact.
- Bedtime:
  - Setting the alarm.
  - Taking the responsibility for waking the other members of the family (be explicit and explain to the child if you think you need to set the alarm for ten minutes after their alarm to be sure everyone is up).
  - Taking charge of making sure other people stick to their bedtime routine (as long as control between siblings is equally distributed).

- ○ Choosing the book for a bedtime story.
- ○ Choosing whether you come upstairs and read them a story or you just tuck them in.
- Incidental details:
  - ▪ 'Should I close the curtains?'
  - ▪ 'Should I put the nightlights on?'
  - ▪ 'Should I shut the door?'

The allowing control techniques can incorporate the vast majority of activities; the chosen activity doesn't have to be one that has become a preoccupation for the child. The aim is that giving the child control over a selection of things that they can manage appropriately should diminish their need to have control in other areas.

There may be tasks that children want to have control over that would be harmful to them. For these activities carers may find *contained control* useful.

Contained control

Contained control requires negotiation between carer and child; this should be done in a way that uses the child's high levels of responsibility and fosters their ability to make decisions.

For any contained control activity the carer and child should make a chart together (see Figure 7.3) that specifies who will have control of which aspects. It is very important that the child has control of more aspects than the carer does; this can be done by drawing out lots of detailed elements of the task if need be. The child can decide on the order of the elements, the colour of the chart, the pictures that are used, etc. Carers can actively defer to the child's decisions on these issues. The chart should then be printed and laminated. It is important for the carer to support their child in making sure that everyone else in the house pays attention to the chart.

In this case David is the child who likes to control.

Figure 7.3 Example of a contained control schedule

Preventative empathic commentary

There will always be things that carers cannot give their children control over, whilst still parenting them responsibly, for example, whether or not they run across a busy road or whether they continue to kick their sister. Such cases present great opportunities for carers to support their child in tolerating their lack of control and thereby assisting the child in developing some trust in their relationship with their carer.

The best strategy on these occasions is empathic commentary. This technique will help children to cope with the emotional turmoil, for example, anger, fear, loss of role, change of rules, that is inherent for them in a lack of control.

Box 7.8 Things to remember about wrestling for control

Understanding how the controlling behaviour makes sense:

- The instinct, for many, when dealing with controlling behaviour in children is either to wrestle control away from the child (along the 'give them an inch and they'll take a mile' principle) or to give up and cede all control to the child.
- Control and responsibility are two sides of the same emotional coin.
- Children who feel compelled to control are used to having to deal with the overwhelming responsibility of looking after themselves and often for others (parents, siblings, etc.).
- The compulsion to control develops due to aversive experiences of others having control (and its resulting in neglect or abuse).
- A child's controlling behaviour comes as an adaptive response to early experiences of having to force the world to meet their needs and keep them safe.
- Others having control can trigger sensory trauma memories of a child's earlier experiences.
- The adaptive strategy to control others becomes hard-wired when it is needed consistently in infancy.
- Dealing with the controlling behaviour of developmentally traumatised children using reward-punishment strategies results in increasing the child's levels of shame due to the child's disconnected and inaccurate sense of responsibility.

Understanding what to do

- EBM for carers:
  - Responsive strategies:
    - A good understanding for a carer of what their own emotional reactions are likely to be can help them to be calmer and less judgemental of their own reactions.

- Carers should not try to deny or mask their feelings but understand them and work with them.
- The Tug of War Alarm.
  - ◦ Preventative strategies:
    - Carers should work on developing an awareness of their reactions to controlling behaviour.
- EBM for children:
  - ◦ Responsive strategies:
    - Responsive Empathic Commentary.
  - ◦ Preventative strategies:
    - Allowing control.
    - Contained control.
    - Preventative empathic commentary.

CHAPTER 8

Lying

Carers often feel manipulated when children apply their previously learned coping strategies to their new homes. Lying is one of the most explicit ways for children to manage their relationships and people's perceptions of them. Carers can find this strategy very difficult to make sense of, and deal with, as there is a tendency to regard honesty and trust as the fundamental cornerstones of meaningful relationships. Deception is very challenging because it undermines those dearly held relationship assumptions.

In the following chapter the lies that traumatised children tend to tell will be grouped into three different types. Each type has particular functions and explanations, which help to make sense of the lies and therefore how they can be approached with children. I will also help carers to think through the ways in which the stories can provide a rich source of information about the truth of a child's 'reality'. The understanding that reality, for many of our children, is not fixed but rather fluid and adaptable, leads to the use of inverted commas around the word 'lie' to suggest that whilst the stories can be seen as lies, they may also contain heavy elements of 'truth'.

Examples
False allegations
Many carers will have experienced the horrifying experience of having an allegation made against them by a child that they're looking after. These can be the most damaging 'lies' for adult-child relationships but they can also do damage due to systemic difficulties in managing the 'lies' as expressions of trauma in relationships. There is often the overly simplistic assumption that either the child is lying through malice or the carer has abused them. This issue is made even more difficult to manage because of the importance, for their emotional well-being, that the accurate disclosures of already traumatised children are believed.

The important nuances to add to this rather simplistic approach to allegations are, first, that children may make false allegations about their carer believing them to be true. In such cases the allegations may have derived from a dissociative re-experiencing of a trauma memory. Second, abusive and/or neglectful relationship dynamics may emerge in a child-carer relationship due to complex relationship replication processes, which have been created by the child's earlier traumatic relationship(s). Ultimately any abusive and/or neglectful experiences must be addressed; however, understanding their cause is crucial in doing so effectively.

The following are examples of allegations made by children that were known to have been false.

Kelly

Kelly was an eight-year-old girl who had lived with her adoptive parents, Jill and Barry, since she was five years old. She had been severely neglected by both of her parents, up until she was taken into care at the age of four years old. Kelly's parents had severe alcohol abuse issues and her father seems to have moved in and out of the home during Kelly's first four years. Her older brother, Gary, frequently hit and kicked Kelly when they fought over the limited amounts of food that were available to them. Her parents also appear to have frequently been involved in physical fights with a variety of visitors to the home. Kelly told me of one occasion on which she had called the police because she was terrified by a fight between her mum and two visitors; this was corroborated by social work records. Kelly had been the one who disclosed the information about the home situation when she started school and had talked openly with a teacher.

Kelly was generally doing well in her adoptive home and bonded well with Barry, her adoptive father. However, she struggled to develop a positive relationship with Jill, her adoptive mother, with whom she argued frequently.

On one occasion Jill had asked Kelly to come in from playing in the garden as it was getting dark. Barry was not around at the time. Kelly had protested vociferously that she wanted to stay outside and Jill had been short-tempered in response. Jill asked Kelly to go upstairs and get changed, as her clothes were dirty; when she refused, Jill guided Kelly towards the stairs by placing a hand on her back. At this point Kelly screamed and shouted, and started having a rage outburst. Jill walked away at this point as she felt that she was not being effective. A few moments later the house fell silent. Jill searched for Kelly, worried about whether she was OK. After a few minutes searching Jill found Kelly curled up under the dining table with the portable telephone. Kelly had called the emergency services and was talking, in an urgent but wavering voice, to the operator telling her that Jill had punched and kicked her.

Jules

Jules was a 15-year-old girl who had lived with her mother and, at different times, several of her mother's partners. She had been sexually abused by at least two of her mother's partners. Jules explained that her mother had known all about the abuse, that it was no secret, and that her mother had dismissed Jules' protests about it.

Jules lived with her single, female foster carer, Bev. Jules had moved to live with Bev nine months prior to my involvement. Since coming into care, aged seven, Jules had had 11 placement moves.

On one occasion Jules and Bev had argued furiously about Jules' refusal to go to school. After quite some time the two had reached a standoff with Jules going to her room and Bev going about her household tasks downstairs.

Unbeknownst to Bev, Jules had barricaded herself in her bedroom by pulling her chest of drawers in front of the door and, after a few hours, had telephoned her social worker and told him that Bev had locked her in the bedroom and prevented her from getting to school. This allegation led to lengthy investigations of Bev's practice and Jules' 'honesty'.

Promoting a useful image

The *promoting a useful image* 'lies' can frequently go unnoticed or become the kind of information that is 'taken with a pinch of salt', for example, 'I scored 16 goals in football today!' or 'Megan fell over and I was the one that got the teacher and everyone said that I was great and wanted to spend all playtime with me.' Sometimes, however, these stories are quite fantastical and can be unrealistic in a way that an adult would rarely believe. This often bewilders and unnerves carers, as it leads them to believe that their child is not just trying to deceive them but also that they are disconnected from reality.

In order to find the reality in such stories it is crucial to look beyond the superficial and examine what problem the lie might solve if it were true or what positive effect it would have for the child if they were to be believed. The following are examples of 'lies' which promote a useful image.

Nathan

Nathan was an 11-year-old boy who had recently been brought into care. He was removed from his family due to allegations that his father had neglected him after Nathan's mother died. It was unclear whether the neglect had preceded his mother's death.

Nathan had lived with his short-term foster carers for four months prior to my involvement. In general terms Nathan seemed to be settling in well; however, he had reportedly been sexually inappropriate with two younger boys in his school. He had responded positively to the safeguards that were put in place in relation to this sexualised behaviour. Nathan's carers had also reported that he frequently told lies. The 'lies' varied in extremity from small white lies to much bigger, quite bizarre lies that his carers could not understand as they did not seem to serve any purpose.

One of Nathan's stories concerned a neighbour's missing bicycle. When Nathan found out about the missing bike he enthusiastically explained to his foster mother that he knew exactly what had happened. Nathan thoughtfully detailed that, from his bedroom window, he had seen a man take the bicycle the previous evening. Nathan went on to explain that he had gone outside and followed the man to an adjacent field where he saw the man bury the bike. Nathan was very keen to be allowed to go and find the bike and bring it back for the neighbour. Nathan's carer was subsequently told that the bike had, in fact, been taken inside by another neighbour in order to protect it.

Ricky

Elements of Ricky's story have appeared in Chapter 7. In addition to his issues with control, detailed in that chapter, Ricky also frequently told 'lies'.

Ricky was a 17-year-old boy who had lived with his mother and, intermittently his father, until coming into care at the age of 11. Since that time he had been through 18 placement moves and at the time that I met Ricky he was in a residential home. Ricky's experience of family life was of brutal violence from his father and neglect from his mother, who was preoccupied by terror and depression. Whilst Ricky was in care all of the people who were important to him, his mother, father and grandmother, had died.

Ricky told lots of 'lies', which had the effect of asserting his control and dominance, that is, he created the impression that he had more information than anyone else. In addition Ricky told some bizarre, fantastical 'lies', in which Ricky was a frightening, violent character that no one would dare to cross. He would proudly tell stories in which his adult cousin, who was a soldier, would get into violently dangerous situations, which he needed to fight his way out of, causing much death and destruction. Ricky would emphasise how close he was to his cousin and how much they enjoyed spending time together. He would also tell stories about his dog, a Staffordshire bull terrier, who he didn't live with, who would bite everyone except him and would attack people on Ricky's command. Ricky's keyworker at his residential home explained that Ricky had not seen any family members and that he did not have a dog.

Protective denial

Protective denial stories are the 'lies' that children tell in order to prevent either being told off or being thought badly of. These are perhaps the easiest 'lies' to recognise and understand, although carers do sometimes become baffled by protective denial stories when carers have no intention of punishing the child for the thing that they are lying about, for example, 'It didn't matter whether she took another biscuit, all the kids were having biscuits, I just asked her how many she had had!'

The following are examples of protective denial 'lies'.

Jonathan

Jonathan was an eight-year-old boy who had been removed from his home after allegations of neglect and sexual abuse relating to him and his younger sister. Jonathan also talked freely about 'having sex' with his sister. There was a suspicion that, although his parents had not successfully stopped the sexual contact between the siblings, his mother had physically chastised Jonathan, very harshly, for the behaviour.

The children's carer, Kath, had used reward-punishment strategies in an attempt to prevent Jonathan from being sexually inappropriate with his sister. After a few weeks of these strategies Jonathan began to deny any behaviour of this kind with his sister.

On one occasion, Kath found Jonathan lying on top of his sister, both of them fully clothed. Kath shouted for Jonathan to move; he quickly jumped up and ran off to his room. After speaking with his sister, Kath went to speak with Jonathan who then acted as though nothing had happened and denied what Kath had seen. Kath reported that Jonathan appeared to be genuinely shocked at the allegation.

Laura

Laura was a 16-year-old girl who had moved into foster care aged 14, having suffered from neglect. Very little was known about her history because her mother, the only significant adult in Laura's life, was unwilling to discuss the issues and denied that there were any problems.

On one occasion Laura was acting sheepishly as she went into the kitchen. Her carer, Paul, got up from what he was doing and curiously followed her and saw that Laura was helping herself to a chocolate bar from the fridge. Laura immediately dropped the chocolate bar, retracted her hand, closed the fridge door and said 'I wasn't taking anything!' Paul quickly said 'No, don't worry, you can have a chocolate bar, it'll be another couple of hours until dinner, help yourself. I was just wondering what was going on, sorry.' Laura responded as though she had been reprimanded and tried very hard to convince Paul that she hadn't been taking anything from the fridge. She was adamant and seemed outraged at the allegation that she felt that Paul was making. Paul continued by saying, 'But I saw you with the chocolate, it's fine though! Take it, it's fine!' Laura persisted with her defence against the perceived allegation and then stormed off into her room and wouldn't speak to Paul or the rest of the family for the entire evening.

Carers' reactions and typical strategies

False allegations

In the face of allegations that carers know to be false, there can be a range of extremely strong emotional reactions. Such allegations not only feel like a betrayal of the trust but also often feel vindictive, cruel and/or rejecting. Furthermore, such allegations can have far reaching implications for foster carers and adoptive parents in the world outside the family, regardless of whether the child intends this or not.

Box 8.1 demonstrates the way in which false allegations can make sense from a child's early history but also illustrates the way in which carers can be invited to replicate the parenting behaviour that precipitated the need.

Box 8.1 Relationship replication: making sense of false allegations

Birth family experience

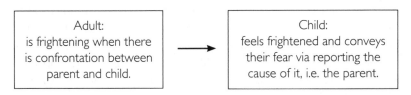

The parent is frightening in their interaction with the child. The child comes to anticipate aggression and therefore feels frightened of the parent when they interact. The child develops a protective strategy of seeking help from others in times of fear by telling others what the parent has done. Whilst frightened the child does not have access to the frontal lobes of the brain and therefore lacks rational reason.

Foster/Adoptive family experience

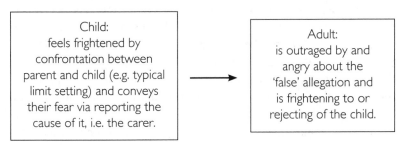

The child has an association of adult–child conflict and aggression/fear and so when conflict, in the form of limit setting combined perhaps with an angry expression on the face of their carer, arises the child is locked in the fear part of their brain and anticipates aggression. As a result the child reports the fear, paired with a legitimate cause for the fear (i.e. an allegation) as a protective strategy. The carer feels outraged and angry about the heinous accusation and is angry and/or rejecting.

SUMMARY: The frightening parenting leads the child to be hypervigilant for aggression and seek help when they see it. The child has unconsciously invited the carer to be frightening/rejecting. The carer has accepted the invitation.

The typical strategies that take hold when a child has made a false allegation about their carer are invariably driven by strong, and entirely understandable, emotional reactions. Carers, in the face of serious allegations, are likely to argue their case and point out that what their child is saying is simply not true. They are also likely to retreat both emotionally and physically resulting in further isolation for the child. Indeed, in the case of foster carers many organisations may recommend that carers start to care for the child in more defensive ways in order to protect them from further allegations. It is not uncommon for the allegations, and the resultant reactions and strategies, to result in placement breakdowns.

Promoting a useful image

Carers can often take 'lies' that promote either a positive or useful image of the child with a 'pinch of salt' and either ignore them or be playful about them. It is, after all, quite typical for a child to exaggerate their success or elevate their own standing in their family.

However, carers do become concerned about these types of 'lies' if they are more fantastical (e.g. Ricky above) or in cases in which the 'lie' causes difficulties with others if it is believed. Carers often respond to such 'lies' by correcting the child and, if that fails, reward-punishment thinking, e.g. reprimand and/or dismissing the child's stories. If these strategies fail then carers can end up arguing, chastising and/or punishing.

Box 8.2 demonstrates the way in which 'lies' that promote a child's image can make sense from their early history. It also demonstrates the way in which carers can be invited to replicate the type of parenting that led to the initial need to 'lie'.

Box 8.2 Relationship replication: making sense of lies that promote a useful image

Birth family experience

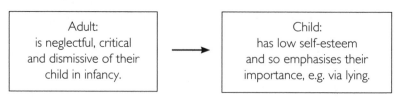

Adult:
is neglectful, critical and dismissive of their child in infancy.

→

Child:
has low self-esteem and so emphasises their importance, e.g. via lying.

The parent is neglectful, critical and/or dismissive of their child. Consequently the child does not feel a sense of specialness and, in order to combat their low self-esteem, emphasises their importance, for example, via lying.

Foster/Adoptive family experience

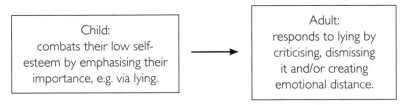

The child uses their strategy of combating their low self-esteem by emphasising their importance, for example, via lying. Their carer knows that the child is lying and so, in the belief that it will help the child to be honest, criticises, dismisses the story and/or creates emotional distance from the child.

SUMMARY: The neglectful, critical and/or dismissive parenting leads the child to need to promote their self-image. The child has unconsciously invited the carer to be critical and/or dismissive. The carer has accepted the invitation.

Protective denial

Carers can often spot and understand protective denial 'lies' more easily than some of the others, particularly when the 'lie' follows a situation in which the child might be reprimanded (for example in the case of Jonathan, above).

It is often more challenging for carers to understand why children would lie when their carers have no intention of reprimanding them. The carer may even go to great lengths to reassure the child that they don't need to lie because they haven't done anything wrong (for example, in the case of Laura and Paul, above). In extreme examples carers can become defensive. They may feel the need to defend themselves against the implied allegation that they would punish their child for something so minor, for example, in the case of Laura; after their confrontation Paul may have become annoyed with Laura as she seemed to imply that he was a mean carer because he wouldn't let her have a chocolate bar.

Defensiveness on the part of carers in the case of such 'lies' may lead them to argue their point and reprimand the child for such behaviour, for example, 'Why on earth have you shouted at me and stormed off? I said you could have the chocolate bar!' This can lead to distance in the relationship, for example, Paul may be similarly irritated and unwilling to speak with Laura.

Box 8.3 demonstrates the way in which 'lies' that children use to protect themselves from reprimand can be understood in light of their early history but also shows the way in which carers can be invited to replicate the parenting in which the need to 'lie' arose.

Box 8.3 Relationship replication: making sense of protective denial

Birth family experience

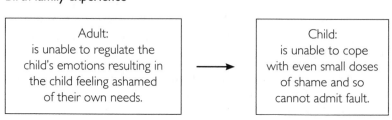

The parent is unable to regulate the child's emotions due to their misattunement or lack of attunement, which shames the child (see Chapter 1). The child is unable to cope with even small doses of shame and so cannot admit fault lest the shame becomes overwhelming.

Foster/Adoptive family experience

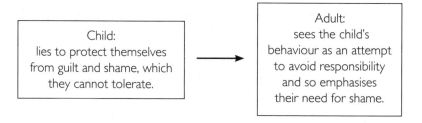

The child, when faced with reprimand for 'bad' behaviour, is unable to cope with the shame that it entails so cannot tolerate admitting fault. Therefore the child may lie in order to protect themselves from the intolerable shame and the damage to their self-esteem that it would cause. The carer sees the child's behaviour as being in need of correction and so, in order for the child to learn from the experience, attempts to convince them of their responsibility, thus shaming the child more.

SUMMARY: The lack of parents' emotional regulation leads to shame and thus a difficulty in tolerating guilt. The child has unconsciously invited the carer to shame them. The carer has accepted the invitation.

Understanding the need to 'lie'

In developing an understanding of why children need to tell lies it is useful to look at the following elements of the EBM model (see Figure 8.1); the need to relate, hard-wired survival strategies, trauma memory, effects of experience on brain and biology, and shame (in bold).

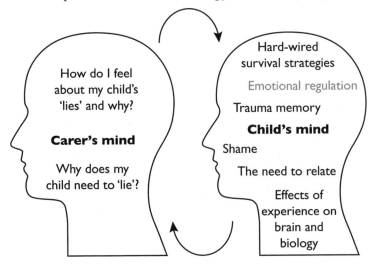

Figure 8.1 EBM model of children who 'lie'

The need to relate and hard-wired survival strategies

Children are bound, trapped even, by their need to relate to other people. This presents two crucial difficulties when seeking to understand why developmentally traumatised children might rely upon telling lies.

First, the person with whom the child relates has an incomparably powerful influence on their developing understanding of reality. Second, a child's need to relate means that, if their primary carer is in some way abusive or neglectful, the child must carefully manage their relationship with that person, whilst simultaneously maintaining it, in whatever way necessary. Unconsciously manipulating reality and their parents' perception of that reality is a very effective strategy for the child to adopt in order to maintain their safety when under stress.

Such behaviour is, of course, developed long before a child is able verbally to construct a 'lie'. However, by the time they develop a capacity for language the child will have already had to become very well versed at controlling their reality.

It is useful to explore the way in which children develop their sense of reality from their primary carer. Often the reality conveyed in the facial expression of abusive and/or neglectful parents is ambiguous or inconsistent. For a baby that face *is* reality; it is the primary way in which infants understand the world. Therefore, if that learned reality is changeable and fluid then a child's way of acting in the world must also be so, in order to accommodate this inconsistency and help to create a reality that is safe.

Second, it is also important to understand an infant's need to manage the relationship with their primary caregiver. If a child repeatedly sees anger, hostility, anxiety or any other emotion that is difficult for a baby to cope with, in the face of their primary carer, then the prime motivator for the infant will be the need to manage the emotion and behaviour of the carer (see the still face exercise in Chapter 1). Therefore, in the later life of such an infant, lying makes complete sense as a strategy to manage their relational environment.

Developmentally traumatised children's understanding of reality is frequently made more confusing as a result of moving between completely different 'realities', that is, home environments. Such children have come from one reality, an environment that was dictated by their parents' behaviour, into another reality in which people behave and, often, think very differently. The previous belief in the ultimate authority of their parents is severely challenged. Children who make this type of journey are therefore well versed in co-ordinating more than one reality at a time but, in order to achieve this feat of mental gymnastics, they need to manage carefully the adults with whom they come into contact.

Trauma memory and effects of experience on brain and biology

In the case of false allegations and protective denial 'lies' it is very likely that the brain of a developmentally traumatised child is reacting to a trauma memory.

This is most apparent in relation to false allegations. In the case of Kelly, the confrontation with her carer and the physical contact of a touch on her back had sparked a disembodied and, in all likelihood, entirely sensory and non-verbal memory of some earlier experience. She was immediately propelled into the primitive, fear and survival, parts of her brain and behaved in accordance with a recalled terrifying experience in which she was compelled to protect herself by seeking help from others.

Kelly's example is a reasonably severe one, in which carer and child had reached quite a significant level of conflict. However, trauma memories may be triggered by more minor altercations.

The brain of a developmentally traumatised child operates on a 'better safe than sorry' basis. Therefore if the child identifies that there is an imminent threat, using the detection system for this that was developed in infancy, the child will act on it. It would, after all, be far too risky for the child to allow themselves to forget about the potential danger and lose the skills for coping with it. However, they do not lose these skills easily as they have been hard-wired into their brain.

Shame

Shame is probably the most important of the model elements when seeking to understand the developmentally traumatised child's need to 'lie'.

Invariably when children 'lie', particularly in the case of promoting a useful image and protective denial, they are seeking to cover up something about themselves that causes them shame. In the examples above, shame played a part in the following ways.

Nathan, in his tale about the bicycle, was attempting to overcome the shame of his negative self-image, particularly his new carers' perception of him as behaving in sexually inappropriate ways. He was unconsciously striving to be seen as valuable, good and, ironically, trustworthy.

Ricky's stories about violence were attempts to mask his crippling self-loathing. He was incredibly ashamed of himself for being unable to protect himself and his mother from his father's violence. He carried the image of himself as weak and cowardly and so fought, very effectively, to create a reality in which he was dominant and frightening in order to avoid his shame.

Jonathan denied his sexualised behaviour with his sister. It may be tempting to assume that Jonathan would do this in order to avoid punishment, which may indeed be the case; however, if this were the exclusive reason then his strategy would not have been to deny something that his carer had witnessed. He would have attempted to excuse his behaviour, blame his sister or explain it away in some other way. Instead he 'lied' and denied it completely. In doing so he was attempting to alter the perceived reality of himself and others around him because he could not tolerate the reality that he was in fact doing something that disgusted the adults he trusted and that was so abhorrent that it might force him to view himself as truly disgusting.

In the case of Laura and the chocolate bar, it is unlikely that she was defending herself against the possibility of punishment, as it was made clear to her that she was not in any trouble. However, Paul's assertions that she was welcome to have the bar of chocolate could do nothing, in the short term, to impact on Laura's own sense of shame. This was shame that Laura felt about responding to her urges, urges that she had learned from her parents' behaviour to be unimportant, excessively demanding and to be ignored.

Children often use 'promoting a useful image' and 'protective denial' lies in order to prevent their carers from finding out about what they unconsciously believe to be their 'true' 'badness'. The fear that the truth will out is so overwhelming that such children must work very hard to ensure that their lie is convincing and sustained.

Consequences of using reward-punishment strategies with children's 'lies'

Many of the 'lies' that developmentally traumatised children tell have specific functions and relate to their hard-wired attempts at survival. These functions relate to their self-esteem, ability to present a safe image, the triggering of trauma memory, the escape from crippling shame and preserving the fragile positive regard of others. The typical strategies that would be used with children who lie, and the instinctive reactions we have to such lies, are not designed to deal with these complex causes and functions and so they cannot possibly deal with them effectively.

If we use typical strategies and reactions, that is, stick with a rigid idea of a singular 'reality', rather than multiple, subjective realities, by confronting the child about their 'lie' without understanding their own perceptions of truth and meaning in the 'lie', then we will only exacerbate the problem.

More tangibly, the main issues that are caused by using reward-punishment thinking in these situations are damage to the adult–child relationship, increase in shame and therefore defensiveness, and increase in the fragility of the child's self-esteem.

With regard to the adult-child relationship, reward-punishment thinking often increases conflict, and decreases empathy and affection in the relationship. The child is likely to fight to maintain the crucial function of their 'lie' when it is disputed, for example, maintaining self-esteem or protecting their safety strategy.

Another problem with using reward-punishment thinking to deal with 'lies', when they serve to avoid shame, is that the child's levels of shame will increase when the child is reprimanded or sanctions are put in place. This is likely to increase the child's defensive behaviour. In other words, if a child is confronted with the existence of a 'lie' that is being used to protect the fragile, positive elements of their self-image they are likely to feel worse about themselves and increase the efforts to ensure the lie is believed.

Empathic behaviour management strategies for children who lie
EBM for carers
RESPONSIVE EBM FOR CARERS
Dealing with false allegations
As I have discussed above, false allegations can be horrifically stressful for carers and generate some very challenging emotions. Carers' first, very understandable, reaction may be about how the allegation will impact on them. There is, after all, a scary world of judgement and condemnation out there. As a result, it is important to nurture, understand and deal with carers' emotions and reactions first, before we can hope to have any empathy for the child who has caused these feelings.

It is very important that carers can evidence the fact that they have done nothing wrong. If there are things that carers would have liked to have done differently, then they should be clear and precise about what these are and what they can do to avoid repeating these things in the future.

Carers can use the information and techniques in Chapter 2 to help them to understand and work through their own feelings and use their 'empathic buddy'.

Until carers can reflect upon and understand their own reactions to allegations the key is for them to try as hard as possible not to get defensive and to try to understand the child's need to make this allegation.

If carers are aware, in advance, that there is a possibility that their child might make allegations about them, and arguably any child that has been through a traumatic early life has the potential to do so, then it is important for carers to work through the preventative strategies below to prepare themselves for how to deal with them when they happen. It is very important that carers work out, in advance, some understandings of why their child may need to make a false allegation, what might provoke it, and what emotional and behavioural reactions it will be likely to invite in the carer.

Searching for the seeds of truth: finding the logical sense in the 'lie'
Box 8.4 contains the details of an exercise for carers, without their child, to help carers to explore the heart of their child's 'lie', what function it serves and how it makes sense. This should help to assuage the negative feelings that carers instinctively feel when they believe that they are being lied to.

Box 8.4 Searching for the seeds of truth: finding the logical sense in the 'lie'

The following are a series of questions for carers to help them to understand the 'lie' that their child has told.

If the story that the child has told was true how would it impact upon the child's life? Would it:

- mean that their behaviour would be justified?
- make the child feel better? If so, why?
- make the child feel that the relationship with their carer is more familiar? If so, why?
- cause someone to rescue the child? If so, why?
- protect the child from thinking badly of themselves?
- make the child feel safer? If so, why?
- prevent carers from thinking badly of their child? If so, why?
- remind the child of something they have previously been made to feel bad about? If so, why?

Having completed the exercise carers should have a better understanding of the value of the 'lie' and why it is important not to dismiss it or reprimand their child for telling the 'lie'. This understanding should also provide invaluable insights for empathic commentary below. This will assist carers to share their newly discovered understandings of their child's inner world with the child.

'Lies' as windows: finding the emotional truth in the 'lie'
Rather than becoming preoccupied with whether or not something a child says is true in an objective, verbal sense, it is useful to work out where the emotional, instinctive truth is, in the 'lie'. To do this it is important to discover the emotional themes of the 'lie'. Gaining this understanding will help to increase the positivity and empathy in carers' relationship with their children and assist with their empathic commentary see Box 8.5.

Carers may find the questions in Box 8.5 useful in helping them to work out the emotional truth of their child's 'lies'.

Box 8.5 'Lies' as windows: finding the emotional truth in the 'lie'

- What were the emotions that your child appeared to be feeling whilst they were telling the 'lie'?
  - Anger?
  - Fear?
  - Disgust?
  - Joy? Etc.
- What were the emotions that you felt while you were hearing the 'lie'?
- What were the emotions that you felt when you found out it was a 'lie'? This and the preceding question will help you to understand what emotional dynamics the child might be unconsciously trying to recreate from their early experience.
- What was the theme of the 'lie'? Understanding this will help you to think about what the child's preoccupation may have been when telling the 'lie' and therefore what is likely to trigger them to 'lie' in the future. The child may have had long relationships with such themes.
  - Blame (e.g. Laura, Jonathan).
  - Danger (e.g. Ricky, Nathan).

- ○ Violence (e.g. Ricky).
- ○ Cruelty (e.g. Kelly, Jules).
- ○ Heroism (e.g. Nathan).
- ○ Threat (e.g. Kelly, Jules).
- ○ Loss (e.g. Nathan).
- ○ Powerful/responsible children (e.g. Ricky, Kelly, Jules), etc.
- Does the 'lie' imply any of the expectations of the child? Or reveal any understandings that the child may have of the world?
  - ○ 'Adults will punish me and I won't be able to handle it.' (e.g. Jonathan)
  - ○ 'Adults think I'm stupid/worthless/lazy/nasty unless I make sure they believe otherwise.' (e.g. Nathan)
  - ○ 'My impulses are bad, therefore I'm bad to act on impulse.' (e.g. Laura, Jonathan)
  - ○ 'I'm not safe unless I keep myself safe.' (e.g. Kelly, Ricky, Jules) etc.

PREVENTATIVE EBM FOR CARERS

Preparing for false allegations

Because they are so challenging to the relationships between developmentally traumatised children and their carers it is particularly important that carers prepare for false allegations in an attempt to take as much of the emotional sting out of them as possible. The guidelines in Box 8.6 may help.

Box 8.6 Preparing for false allegations: guidelines

- Carers should talk as much as they can with relevant professionals, e.g. supervising social workers about:
  - ○ the potential for allegations
  - ○ the occurrence of allegations
  - ○ carers' proposed strategies for dealing with allegations. If carers believe that they need to deal with the allegations as expressions of traumatic memory, by providing the child with an interpretation of the cause of their allegation, e.g. empathic commentary, this should only be done after it has been discussed with relevant professionals. Otherwise it may appear that carers are trying to convince their child to alter their allegation.

- Carers should be ready to accept that allegations will be made and prepare for them.
- Carers should investigate allegations about others, with appropriate professional support and guidance, with as much objectivity and compassion as they can.
- It is useful for carers to prepare themselves for the invitation to act defensively in relation to children's 'lies'.
- Carers can prepare other people for the fact that their child may need to process some of their trauma by saying negative, accusatory things about others when they are extremely stressed/distressed.
- Carers can work towards identifying the potential trigger points for their child's 'lies'. Given the child's past experience, when are they likely to feel the need to protect themselves by calling for the help of others?

Accepting multiple realities

One of the major difficulties in knowing how to deal with 'lies' is that carers often feel that they should be directing children to share a singular static reality. However, as discussed above, this may be more challenging for developmentally traumatised children than for other children due to their need to manage the difficult realities they have lived within.

There are many ways in which adults are perfectly content to accept that life is not as simple as true or false, black or white, but it is often much more challenging when it comes to children telling 'lies'. Carers are primed to believe that they should correct children's behaviour using reward-punishment thinking. If they don't, using this logic, then they would surely be encouraging children to lie. The list in Box 8.7 gives examples of the ways in which adults readily accept and often encourage multiple realities and understandings of the world without fear that they are condoning and encouraging dishonesty.

Box 8.7 Accepting multiple realities

The following are everyday examples in which multiple realities are readily accepted. The 'lies' of traumatised children can be just as useful and 'truthful' as the following.

- *Opinion*: We can quite happily accept subjective opinion without feeling that it threatens our ability to discern it from scientific or evident fact.

- *Subjectivity*: How do we know that the way one person sees the colour yellow is the same as the way that another person sees it?
- *In children's imaginative play*: We do not worry that allowing imaginative play will corrupt children's ability to understand the truth, even when they insist that their play is 'real', e.g. 'The dinosaur really did eat up the train!' Indeed we join in and make the different reality even more real, 'Oh yeah, and now he's going after the truck!'
- *Fantasy*: e.g. in films, plays, drama and the ultimate in joyful, multiple realities, Father Christmas.
- *Hyperbole*: i.e. exaggerations to make a point.
- *Magicians and illusionists*: We are happy to be 'tricked' into believing something that we know cannot be true. It doesn't offend or alarm us as an example of dishonesty.

Overall, it's useful, with traumatised children who 'lie', for carers to accept a more playful, fluid idea of what reality is. It is only through carers doing this, travelling alongside their child's reality, that the child will feel safe enough to abandon their need for multiple realities.

EBM for children

RESPONSIVE EBM FOR CHILDREN

'Lies' as windows to children's emotional worlds

The 'Lies as Windows' exercise for carers (Box 8.5), above, can be adapted to include their child. However, it is useful for carers to have done the exercise first. When it comes to dealing with a 'lie', it is useful for carers to go along with it and be curious. If the 'lie' is shut down, by the carer by them telling their child that it is not true, it is tantamount to pulling the curtains closed on a valuable window into the child's emotional world.

Carers may find the guidelines and questions in Box 8.8 useful when their child has told a 'lie'.

Box 8.8 'Lies' as windows

The following are guidelines to using children's 'lies' as windows into their inner world.

- There is no need for carers to challenge what their child is saying.

- It is important for carers to get excited and curious about the 'lie', e.g. 'Oh wow! What happened next?'
- Carers should pick up on the themes within the 'lies', e.g. 'Wow, you were such a hero!', 'You were really expecting us to fall out about it!'
- Once carers have spent a long time with their child in the reality of their 'lie' they can, if necessary, introduce their reality, e.g. in the case of Leo, 'Oh that's weird, because the neighbours said that he'd taken the bike to keep it safe! Well that's OK, I guess, you both saw different things.' Carers should be careful not to be dominant or contradictory with their own reality; this is simply another stream to the story and, like a story, there does not need to be agreement about the details of it.

Empathic commentary

Empathic commentary can be a very powerful strategy to deal with even the most provocative 'lies'. Carers can follow the Golden Rules (Box 3.9, Chapter 3) and use the example statements in Box 8.9 to help them to come up with their own.

Box 8.9 Responsive empathic commentary for 'lies'

The following statements may be useful for carers in their responses to their child 'lies'.

False allegations

Before using these statements, carers should ensure that they have prepared by discussing the potential for their use with relevant professionals, e.g. their supervising social worker. This will potentially avoid the appearance that carers are trying to change the child's story.

- 'Wow, something happened and it felt for a moment like I was hurting you, like Mummy used to. I never want to hurt you like that.'
- 'It makes me so sad to think that you get frightened of me sometimes but I think it's when I do something that reminds you of how Gary used to treat you.'

Promoting a useful image

- 'Wow, it sounds like you are a real hero in that story! I wonder if you need to make sure I know how brave you are!'

- 'You're telling me about so many scary things that happened at school today and what a tough person you are. I wonder if making people feel that you're a scary boy helps to make you feel safe!'

Protective denial

- 'I'm so sorry that I have to stop you hitting your brother; I know you really want to be in charge of him. I also think that you want to make sure that I won't stop loving you. It must feel really horrible when I see you do something like that and tell you off. I bet it makes you feel even worse about yourself and maybe even that I won't love you any more.'

- 'Gosh, you're telling me that you didn't take the chocolate even though I saw you do it! That's confusing. I wonder if it's because you believe that I'll think you're a terrible person. I'll never think that of you, even if you do something that I'm not keen on!'

PREVENTATIVE EBM FOR CHILDREN

Prepare for the 'lie'

When things are calm and carer and child have an opportunity to chat together it can be invaluable to prepare for the 'lies' that will happen in the future.

The understandings developed in the exercises above can assist carers to communicate to their child that they have got some good ideas about why their child's 'stories' or 'lies' sometimes need to be told.

Carer and child can prepare together for when the fear of harm, the need to promote a useful image and the need to protect from shame might take over. Also, they can think and talk together about how they will know when the child has those fears and what the child could do instead of 'lying'. If the carer and child cannot find alternatives then they can reach an agreement to accept what the child says as explaining something about how they're feeling and that the carer will do their best to help the child to feel better.

Preventative empathic commentary

Carers can use responsive empathic commentary to help prevent future 'lies'. They should wait for a calm, happy time when carer and child can sit together and have a meaningful conversation without worrying about heightened emotions.

Carers should follow the Golden Rules (Box 3.9, Chapter 3) and use the example statements in Box 8.10 to enable them to develop their own statements.

Box 8.10 Preventative empathic commentary for 'lies'
False allegations
Before using this type of statement, carers should ensure that they have prepared by discussing the potential for its use with relevant professionals for example, their Supervising Social Worker. This will potentially avoid the appearance that carers are trying to change the child's story.

'You know when you got really upset with me yesterday and it really felt like I pulled your arm too hard and pulled you on to the floor? And you know that I got confused because I didn't think that I had hurt you! Well, I had a brilliant idea this morning about what happened! I was wondering whether, when you stopped to look in the shop window and I carried on, it felt a bit like when Dad used to push you around and hurt you and you got really frightened that I would do the same thing. I'm so sorry that I scared you.'

Promoting a useful image
'Do you remember yesterday when you told me about the neighbour's bike and how you could go and find it for him? I was wondering whether it feels really nice when you get to tell me about really impressive, heroic things that you've done! I love hearing about those kinds of things! I bet you haven't had much of a chance to feel really special with many other adults. I'm really sorry about that. I want to make you feel really special and loved.'

Protective denial
'You know yesterday when we ended up falling out about the chocolate bar? I'm so sorry that happened. I've been thinking about it, because I found it really confusing. I wondered if you were worried that I would tell you off. Maybe Mum and Dad didn't let you have things that you needed and wanted so maybe you felt embarrassed, as if you shouldn't have even gone in the fridge. I'm so sorry I made you feel like that. I really want to make you feel happy and at home here.'

Box 8.11 Things to remember about 'lies'

Understanding how the 'lies' make sense

- 'Lies' that developmentally traumatised children tell can be seen as containing much more truth than might be initially assumed.
- The 'lies' can be grouped into three main types:
  - false allegations
  - promoting a useful image
  - protective denial.
- False allegations often occur as a result of a need to sabotage a potential close relationship with a carer when closeness does not feel safe.
- False allegations can also occur when a trauma memory is triggered by a confrontation or some other stressful situation and the child acts as though they are actually under the threat of the triggered memory.
- 'Lies' that promote a useful image can occur when a child has low self-esteem and they feel the need to prevent someone from seeing what they believe to be their 'real' 'bad' self.
- 'Lies' that promote a useful image can also occur when a child feels that image of themselves will keep them safe and deter anyone that may want to harm them.
- Protective denial 'lies' usually occur when a child feels the need to avoid blame or responsibility as the shame that they already feel is too great for them to tolerate.
- Reward-punishment strategies often lead children who 'lie' due to the impact of their developmental trauma to increase their 'lying' to maintain their hard-wired survival strategies, persuade carers of their self-worth and prevent intolerable shame.

Understanding what to do

- EBM for carers:
  - Responsive strategies:
    - A good understanding for a carer of what their own emotional reactions are likely to be can help them to be calmer and less judgemental of their own reactions.
    - Carers should not try to deny or mask their feelings but understand them and work with them.
    - Dealing with false allegations.

- Searching for the seeds of truth: finding the logical sense in the 'lie'.
  - 'Lies' as windows: finding the emotional truth in the 'lie'.
  - Preventative strategies:
    - Carers should work on developing an awareness of their reactions to 'lies'.
    - Preparing for false allegations.
    - Accepting multiple realities.
- EBM for children:
  - Responsive strategies:
    - 'Lies' as windows to your child's emotional world.
    - Responsive empathic commentary.
  - Preventative strategies:
    - Prepare for the 'lie'.
    - Preventative empathic commentary.

CHAPTER 9

Sexualised Behaviour

The sexualised behaviour of children is an incredibly difficult subject for adults to think about and reflect upon openly. As a result it is often avoided or dealt with in a relatively superficial, behavioural manner rather than in an emotional one. The reasons for this are complex but usually centre on cultural and societal difficulties in being open about sexuality in general, but in particular our reticence about the sexuality of children (when relevant) and younger teenagers. There are particular difficulties when children direct their sexual attention towards adults and further anxieties are generated when thinking about children who focus their sexual urges on other children. Another challenge when considering sexualised behaviour in children traumatised by abuse and/ or neglect is the frequent need to juggle the simultaneous identities of a child as both victim and perpetrator. This is all in addition to attempting to understand what typical sexual development and behaviour in children and teenagers is.

The sexualised behaviour commonly seen in traumatised children can be grouped into three categories. Some children display sexualised behaviour towards adults, some towards other children (most frequently their siblings) and some display sexualised behaviour alone but are indiscriminate about who sees them.

Examples of sexualised behaviour

'Sexualised behaviour', 'inappropriate sexual behaviour', 'children who sexually harm' and 'sexual abuse' are all terms that are used to describe the issues that will be explored in this chapter. The problem with the use of such cursory labels is that they are often used in lieu of an adequate description of the behaviour that has occurred. The, often deeply uncomfortable, specifics of children's sexualised behaviour are essential elements in helping us to understand it.

In the following examples I have attempted to provide details of a range of sexualised behaviours in order to demonstrate the power and usefulness of the nuanced specifics. The examples also include information about the associated conduct that often goes alongside overt sexualised behaviour, for example, invasions of personal space and heightened interest and arousal at sexual themes on TV.

Sexualised behaviour towards adults

Emma and Christie

Emma, who was nine years old, and Christie, her six-year-old sister, had been taken into local authority foster care seven months prior to my involvement. The girls had been neglected, had witnessed their parents having sex and had spent a great deal of time without adult supervision. Their mother was dependent upon illegal drugs and their father was rarely in the family home. Since coming into care Emma had made some allusions to 'laying down' with her father but at the time there had been no direct indication that the girls had been sexually abused.

Their carers, Bill and Mary, had reported that the girls appeared happy and settled and were fun to have around. However, the carers also said that the girls would frequently sit uncomfortably close to them and appeared to have no understanding of personal space boundaries. Mary noted that the girls were willing and able to ask her for a hug but that on one occasion, when Mary was hugging Christie, she had casually left her hand on Mary's breast and then made eye-contact with her and smiled. Mary felt very uncomfortable about this and believed that Christie was in some way asking Mary whether that was what she wanted. Mary stated that she also felt occasionally uncomfortable about what felt like lingering touches from the girls.

Mary also reported that Emma seemed to be very interested in Mary's 26-year-old nephew, Tom, who frequently visited the house. Mary explained that when Tom was due to visit Emma would want to dress in short skirts and tiny tops. She would also make a bee-line to sit next to Tom, touch his arm, giggle at what he said and would try to exclude others from the conversation. This behaviour, understandably, made Tom feel very uncomfortable.

Bill explained that when the girls had first arrived, he would read them a story at bedtime before tucking them in for the night. He described one occasion on which he had gone to give Christie a kiss on the forehead. He reported that she had instinctively gone to kiss him on the mouth and had opened her mouth.

Sexualised behaviour towards other children

Nathan

Nathan was an 11-year-old boy who had recently been brought into care when I became involved. He was removed from his family due to allegations that his father had neglected him after Nathan's mother died. It was unclear whether the neglect had preceded his mother's death. It had been reported that Nathan had behaved in 'sexually inappropriate ways' towards two younger boys in his school.

In the first incident Nathan, aged nine at the time, had reportedly followed a seven-year-old boy into the toilet and shown him his penis whilst telling the boy to touch it. In the second incident, involving a boy of six years old when Nathan was ten, Nathan was reported to have asked the boy, in a secluded part of the playground, whether the boy wanted Nathan to 'put my willy [penis] in your bum'. On both occasions Nathan appeared to have taken 'no' for an answer but had tried to persuade the boys not to tell anyone.

Jonathan

Jonathan's story, first mentioned in Chapter 8, is also relevant in this chapter. In this instance there were clearly attempts by Jonathan to engage in sexual activity with his younger sister. There were also incidents that appeared to have been reciprocal. Jonathan freely described that his sister would 'suck his willy' and he would put his 'fingers into her bum'. I hesitate to say that the acts were 'consensual'; however, it did appear that neither child had considered protesting.

Kai

Kai was a five-year-old boy who had been severely neglected. When I knew him Kai had been living in a foster placement for the previous two years. Before coming into care, Kai's mother, who had alcohol issues, frequently left Kai alone in his cot for days at a time.

In addition to rage outbursts and attachment-seeking, Kai was also reported to be displaying some 'sexually inappropriate behaviour' at school. Kai would frequently chase girls around in class and in the playground. His teacher described that he would deliberately try to grab their bottoms, put his hand up their skirts and grab their genitalia. The teachers also reported that the behaviour had not decreased even though they had explained to him that he should not do it, monitored him closely at playtimes and started to remove his privileges.

Public displays of sexualised behaviour
Jess
Jess was a three-year-old girl who had been in foster care for ten months. She had been removed from the care of her parents due to neglect and witnessing domestic violence.

Jess had settled into her placement well and appeared to have bonded very well with her foster carers. However, they were concerned about Jess' gleefully aggressive behaviour towards other children and one reported incident of sexualised behaviour. The incident had occurred when her foster mother, Toni, had gone into Jess' room one morning to get her out of bed. They had spent a brief time playing with the dolls and cuddly toys that Jess had by her bed. Jess was enjoying the play, smiling and giggling with Toni. In the same giggly mood, Jess reportedly placed one of the dolls on her bed, moved on to her hands and knees and proceeded to wiggle her tongue up and down between her doll's legs, then make eye-contact with Toni and giggle coyly.

Pavan
I became involved with Pavan when she was 11 years old. At the time she was in a long-term foster placement with her carer, Suki. Pavan was an only child and had been severely neglected by her parents. Her father had left the family home and her mother suffered from paranoid delusions about Pavan that led her to lock Pavan, almost permanently, in her room.

Pavan had a mild learning disability. Suki explained to me that her main concern was that Pavan would 'masturbate' frequently with little regard for who was around her. Suki had explained to Pavan that what she was doing was private but this had not been effective in reducing the behaviour as Pavan appeared simply to ignore Suki's comments. Suki was also concerned that the frequency of the behaviour might result in soreness that might exacerbate the behaviour.

When I asked Suki to describe what she meant when she talked about 'masturbation' she described that Pavan would 'fumble around in her underwear' and that she would sometimes become red-faced and very intense. Suki said that Pavan would also absent-mindedly rock on the edges of chairs, seemingly in order to stimulate herself.

Typical strategies

It is common for adults to react to the sexualised behaviour of children with reward-punishment thinking. Responding empathically to such behaviour requires us to accept, and think in great detail about, the sexual thoughts and feelings of children. It may also necessitate thoughts about the origin of such behaviour, for example, sexual abuse, domestic violence, exposure to sexually explicit materials and challenges the comforting idea that 'good' and 'bad' can be neatly separated and defined: that is, it demonstrates that sexual vulnerability and predatory sexual behaviour can exist simultaneously in the same person. In addition, accepting the potential vulnerability and innocence of someone that could do something so abhorrent can also causes us shame, 'How can I love and accept someone who could sexually assault a child? What does that say about me?'

There are two enticing options that a person's unconscious might take in order to by-pass this internal conflict, first, to avoid or minimise the sexualised behaviour or, second, to allow or create emotional distance from the child (Boxes 9.1 and 9.2).

Box 9.1 Relationship replication: Sexualised behaviour
Birth family experience

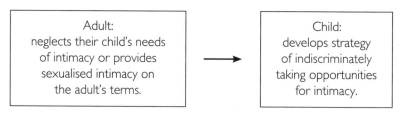

Adult: neglects their child's needs of intimacy or provides sexualised intimacy on the adult's terms.	Child: develops strategy of indiscriminately taking opportunities for intimacy.

The parent is unable to meet their child's need for appropriate physical and emotional intimacy. The child develops a strategy for having their need for intimacy met by taking the opportunities that arise for closeness with other people or in situations that are otherwise inappropriate. This may escalate into vulnerability for sexual exploitation.

Foster/Adoptive family experience

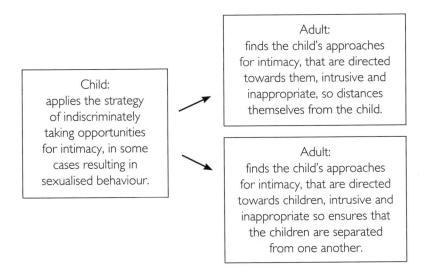

The child applies an indiscriminate strategy for achieving closeness with adults, possibly including an expectation that the offer of intimacy may be conditional, that is, that the child should allow themselves to be sexually exploited. The carer deals with the 'inappropriate' sexual behaviour by ensuring that their (appropriate) intimacy could not be misinterpreted and distances the child from them and others.

SUMMARY: The sexualised or neglectful parenting leads the child indiscriminately to seek intimacy. The child has unconsciously invited the carer to restrict their access to physical and emotional intimacy. The carer has accepted the invitation.

Box 9.2 Relationship replication: sexualised behaviour (domestic violence)

Birth family experience

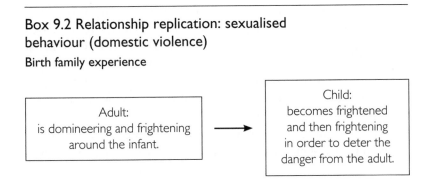

The parent is frightening in their behaviour around the infant, including being domestically violent. The child is preoccupied by fear and becomes frightening and domineering in order to deter the threat. Intimate relationships become marked by fear, threat and domination.

Foster/Adoptive family experience

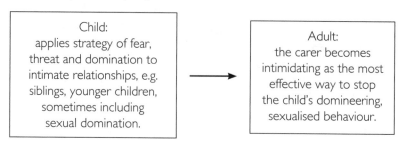

The child applies their understanding of relationships, that is, that they are marked by fear, domination and intimidation to their interactions with their carer and other children. In the absence of experiences of appropriate intimacy in infancy the child may engage in sexually harmful behaviour towards other children.

SUMMARY: The frightening/domineering parenting leads the child to be frightened and frightening. The child has unconsciously invited their carer to be domineering and intimidating. The carer has accepted the invitation.

In practical terms carers may first attempt to explain to their child why they should not engage in such sexualised behaviour and then reprimand them for further transgressions. When this strategy is applied to children who engage in sexualised behaviour with other children it requires that the adult be sure of who the 'perpetrator' is. Often, in my experience, when there is sexual behaviour between different genders, it is typically the male child who is considered to be the 'perpetrator' and the female is identified as the 'victim'. However, sexualised siblings can engage in sexual behaviour without either of them being a 'perpetrator' or 'victim' in this black and white sense, for example, Jonathan and his sister (above). Child sexualised behaviour can be an enormously complex issue as there may also be coercion, acquiescence and ambivalence to consider.

Ultimately many children who display sexualised behaviour suffer devastating punishments for their behaviour, that is, they are moved from their placements, communities, schools and/or their sibling(s). These things are rarely done as an overt punishment, but due to the pervasive nature of reward-punishment thinking they are frequently considered to be the best option. In some cases of course the very difficult decision has to be made to compromise the attachment needs of one child in order to ensure the safety of another.

Another common, and very understandable, strategy is to reduce the levels of intimacy in the caregiving and sibling relationships. This enables the risk to another child to be managed and hopefully reduced and reduces the risk that a child will make a false allegation against their carer.

However, with developmentally traumatised children, all of these consequences will increase the levels of shame, attachment-seeking behaviours and need for the use of hard-wired survival strategies and so should be avoided if at all possible.

Understanding sexualised behaviour

The elements of the 'child's mind' part of the EBM model (Figure 9.1) that are most pertinent when seeking to understand the sexualised behaviour of developmentally traumatised children are the need to relate, emotional regulation, effects of experience on brain and biology and shame (in bold).

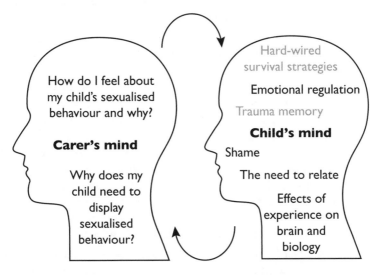

Figure 9.1 EBM model of sexualised behaviour

The need to relate

There are several types of early experience that can drive a child's need to present in a sexualised manner. It is tempting to assume that all children who display sexually inappropriate behaviour have been sexually abused in their past. Whilst this is often proved to be the case, and indeed may still be the case even when sexual abuse is not disclosed, there are other experiences that can lead to sexualised behaviour (Box 9.3).

Box 9.3 Infant experiences that make sense of sexualised behaviour

Prolonged exposure to any of the following can help to make sense of children finding comfort, satisfaction and/or safety in sexualised behaviour.

- *Neglect*: For infants, the lack of physical and mental stimulation and emotional regulation can lead a child to need to self-stimulate and self-regulate, simply as a way of achieving some form of mental activity.

- *Misattuned, intrusive care*: If an infant's instinctive need to protect their personal space is consistently overridden by someone more powerful, the infant learns to override the instinct. For example, an infant's signals about their preferences regarding touch and/or interaction are ignored or disregarded, being forcibly fed when not hungry, being picked up roughly when asleep, being kissed or touched despite turning away or protesting. Consequently they become incapable of applying personal space boundaries to themselves or others.

- *Sexual abuse*: This is linked with the acceptance of being intruded upon (intrusive care). If the desires of the adult, or more powerful child, persistently take precedence over the needs/preferences/protests of the child then the child will learn to override their own expression, and perhaps their own perception, of personal boundaries.

- *Neglect and sexual abuse*: Children who have been neglected but then gain access to some affection through a sexually abusive adult or child will learn to suppress any internal protest regarding the sexual abuse in order to gain access to the conditional affection. This can result in them taking this idea of conditional love/affection into future relationships with adults and other children, thus leaving them unable to apply the need for personal space boundaries to themselves and others and making them vulnerable to abusive adults.

- *The anger/fear of self and/or others*: If a baby learns to accept that their fear, discomfort, pain, etc. is disregarded by others they will learn to disregard it themselves and then struggle to apply consideration of those elements to others, e.g. physical abuse or domestic abuse. Therefore the themes of the experience, e.g. domination, cruelty and humiliation, may become accepted ways of relating to others and potentially take the form of sexually inappropriate behaviour towards them.

It is important to note that whilst certain types of early trauma may lead to sexualised behaviour, that trauma may also be expressed in other behaviours that are not overtly sexual, for example, rage, intrusiveness of other kinds, nosiness, personal space issues, seeking affection indiscriminately.

In short, the nature of the developmentally traumatic experience is likely to be echoed in the nature of the sexualised behaviour. In order properly to understand what drives the sexualised behaviour we must understand it in its nuanced detail and what pleasures and/or irresistible impulses are at work. It is for this reason that, when we see labels of 'sexualised behaviour', 'sexually inappropriate behaviour' or 'masturbation', we need to find a way to overcome our visceral disgust, confront the issue and be willing to ask awkward, uncomfortable questions about the details of who, why, where, how and, exactly, what.

Emotional regulation

Children who have not experienced having their emotions regulated in infancy, particularly those that have experienced severe neglect, will have often developed solo strategies that help to regulate their mood. Most people can remember the TV images of the children placed in Romanian orphanages in the early 1990s. These children had very little interaction with adults and almost no responsive interaction that would help them to regulate their emotions. In the absence of a responsive adult many of them used one of the few strategies available to them for regulating themselves, rocking. This rhythmical activity, in the absence of anything else, creates a physiological reaction that will go some way to regulating a child when they need it. We can see these characteristics in the strategies we instinctively use with distressed babies.

'Masturbation' is one such way that some children can break through the numbness of their existence. It is not necessarily sexual but it is, necessarily, intensely sensory and potentially soothing.

Effects of experience on brain and biology

As discussed in Chapter 1, the experience-dependent nature of the pre-frontal cortex of their brains means that children who have experienced developmental trauma are likely to have underdeveloped executive functions. One such executive function is the ability to inhibit impulses. When sexualised children have the urge to seek comfort, self-regulate or simply engage with another person, as any of us might, these children may instinctively look to sexual activity to fulfil those needs. Such children are unlikely, to be able to inhibit their impulse to act on such imperative relational needs.

If a child's sexualised behaviour is due to difficulties with impulsivity then reward-punishment thinking is unlikely to yield positive results.

Shame

Children may not find their sexualised behaviour inherently shameful, even in cases in which the child is actively abusing another child. It is tempting to imagine that if we communicate to the child that their behaviour is unacceptable and make them a little ashamed of it then they are bound to be deterred from doing it again. Indeed this is the tactic that is most commonly applied when dealing with many challenging behaviours of children and its use makes complete sense within the framework of reward-punishment thinking.

As explored in Chapter 1, the problem with the application of shame is that developmentally traumatised children are very poor at handling it and quickly become defensive and protect their own behaviours by hiding them. In addition, sexualised behaviour may enable children to meet their needs for intimacy and so facilitate an important, fundamental drive that a developmentally traumatised child cannot afford to abandon.

Consequences of using reward-punishment thinking with sexualised behaviour

When inherently shaming, reward-punishment strategies are employed to deter developmentally traumatised children from displaying sexualised behaviour the likely consequence will be that the behaviour will be concealed but not that it will be stopped. This is almost certainly the case when these strategies are used without replacing them with alternatives that address the need that has driven the behaviour.

Reducing intimacy, via limiting physical touch and/or separating siblings, may, at first glance, seem like an entirely sensible strategy when dealing with a child who displays sexualised behaviour. It certainly meets the short-term goals of reducing the opportunities for sexualised behaviour. However, it is likely, in children who have already been starved of appropriate intimacy, to increase their drive to seek out the intimacy and adds in the necessity for deception, thus making it much harder to prevent.

Fundamentally we need to communicate to a child, and allow them to internalise the belief, that these behaviours are, in fact, understandable. that the needs which drive the sexualised behaviours (e.g. loneliness, emotional regulation, intimacy) can be accommodated, understood and actually welcomed. If we can achieve this then we can prevent the child's need to sustain their sexualised behaviour into adulthood by whatever means necessary, for example, deception, coercion, exploitation.

Empathic behaviour management strategies

EBM for carers

RESPONSIVE EBM FOR CARERS

Crucially, if there is any potential that there has been illegal behaviour it is important for the legal process that witness statements are taken before carers have the, suggested, detailed conversations with their child.

As detailed earlier in the chapter it is important, for the well-being of the child and the effective management of the behaviour, for carers not to be afraid of the detail of their child's sexualised behaviour. Carers may be able to find out some details by setting up a relaxed non-judgemental conversation with their child. However, if the child is being shamed by the conversation then it's best that the conversation is paused. Carers may be able to find out more information from other sources, children, teachers, etc.

Specific detail of both the sexualised behaviour and the situation in which it occurred will assist carers to understand the motivating force for the behaviour more effectively than the coy simplistic summaries that are commonplace in such instances.

It is important, when carers are responding to children's sexualised behaviour, to focus upon the drive behind the sexualised behaviour.

- What does the child gain from their behaviour? Is it intimacy, comfort, control, dominance, emotional regulation, soothing or some other infantile need?
- Is there anything in the child's history that explains their need?

Carers should focus on answering the questions above in order to avoid the instinct to deny the behaviour or blame and/or distance themselves from the child.

PREVENTATIVE EBM FOR CARERS

It is important for carers to prepare for their own reactions to sexualised behaviour; such reactions can be extremely strong and influence the ways in which the problem is dealt with by carers. There are several ways suggested in Chapter 2; in particular Box 2.12 will allow carers to pre-empt and explore their own individual reactions to sexualised behaviour.

In order for carers to prepare for conversations with their child about the sexualised behaviour it is useful to think ahead of time about what potential subjects might need to be discussed. Carers should spend some time getting used to the sexual language that will feel comfortable for them and their child. It is useful for carers to practise describing sexualised behaviour with their 'empathic buddy' (see Chapter 2) or someone else they trust. It is important to use honest, accurate language that isn't ambiguous; there is a world of coy euphemisms out there for sexual acts and body parts. Whilst it is important that the conversation is comfortable, it is also important that it is clear and straightforward.

Once the initial embarrassment has been dealt with, carers can focus their preparation on trying to think empathically and without judgement about the sexualised behaviour that they might encounter.

EBM for children

RESPONSIVE EBM FOR CHILDREN

It is, clearly, very important for carers to do their best to prevent children from hurting and/or sexually abusing or exploiting any other child and to prevent them from placing themselves in a position in which their sexual vulnerability might be exploited. However, in order to work towards a long-term solution to the sexualised behaviour, it is very important, when responding to it, that carers do not shame their child. Whilst it is important to react assertively, it is just as important to act empathically.

Responsive empathic commentary

When carers have regulated their own emotional reaction, one of the most effective strategies for responding to sexualised behaviour is for carers to commentate on what they think is going on inside their child's mind and body (Box 9.4).

Empathic commentary will help children to read, from their carer's facial expressions, body language and words, an understanding of their own inner worlds and therefore their behaviour. It is from this starting point that a journey towards a change in behaviour can begin.

Box 9.4 Responsive empathic commentary for sexualised behaviour

The following are statements that carers can try in response to sexualised behaviour. Using these as a guideline and the Golden Rules in Box 3.9, Chapter 3, carers can also come up with their own statements.

- 'Oh, I see, you've started rubbing yourself on my knee. I wonder if you think that's what I want when I give you a cuddle!'
- 'Of course you feel like you should touch in between my legs; you didn't really used to get cuddles when you were with Mum and Dad except when Dad wanted to have sex with you! Well that makes what you're doing make complete sense! I want you to be able to have cuddles with me without feeling that you have to do that though. I'll give you cuddles because children need cuddles not because I want to have sex with you.'
- 'I think you want to touch my breasts because that was how you used to get close to Mum. We can be close and have really big hugs without you touching my breasts.'
- 'Wow! You really like the idea of kissing me on the lips with your mouth open. I can completely understand why because that's what you used to do with Mum but it makes me feel a bit uncomfortable. I prefer it when we kiss on the head or on the cheek or on the hand or when we rub noses and have big cuddles.'
- 'You're rubbing your penis, Tom; I wonder if you're feeling worried or bored. I'm not quite sure which. We could read a book together or have a chat so you don't have to worry or be bored or lonely.'
- 'You and Shaun were kissing on the mouth then; I wonder if that felt nice. You and Shaun used to spend so much time together without any grown-ups to look after you properly, you must have got lots of comfort from each other when you didn't get cuddles from Mum or Dad. There are lots of ways you can get comfort from me now, like

by cuddles, or talking, or holding hands, or making cakes together, or playing games together. Kissing on the lips with tongues is for two grown-ups only.'

Substitutes for sexualised behaviour

If carers' understandings of their child lead them to believe that their sexualised behaviour is driven by a need for intimacy then, even though it is a little counterintuitive, it is best to respond to them with (appropriate) intimacy. Of course if there is another child involved it is important to deal with the emotions of that other child first, preferably if there are two carers, then they can deal with one child each at the same time.

When talking to the child who is displaying the sexualised behaviour carers can make a statement along the lines of 'You mustn't lay on top of your sister like that. I understand that you do that when you're feeling lonely. Come and have a cuddle with me but we cuddle and show our affection with our arms and our smiles not with the bits between our legs. I'm so sorry you were feeling lonely. I don't want you to feel lonely!' and then the carer can comfort the child.

PREVENTATIVE EBM FOR CHILDREN

Preventative empathic commentary

The best place to start when attempting to prevent the re-occurrence of sexualised behaviour is for carers to convey to the sexualised child what they have understood about what is going on for the child and why they may be driven to engage in such behaviour (Box 9.5).

Box 9.5 Preventative empathic commentary for sexualised behaviour

The following are statements that carers can try in a calm period to try to prevent their child's need to engage in sexualised behaviour. Using these as a guideline and the Golden Rules in Box 3.9, Chapter 3, carers could also come up with their own statements.

- 'David and Jane are coming over for dinner tonight. You really like it when you get to talk to David (grown-up) all by yourself! That makes sense! I think it makes you feel really special. I wonder if it reminds you of the type of relationship that you and Daddy used to have and the way he made you feel special when you used to touch his penis and he touched your vagina. You *are* really special and I want to show you that but I need to help you feel special without you feeling the need to flirt with grown-ups.'

- 'Your friend Lilly is staying over tonight. I think it might feel really tempting to get into bed with her and touch her like you and Kirsty (sister) used to. I can understand why! It made you feel really close when there was no one else to feel close to! So if you feel like that then come and see me and we can have a lovely cuddle without the need to touch each other on our private parts.'

- 'Guess what I've noticed! I've noticed that when you get bored, like yesterday when you were watching TV, you end up with your hand in your knickers touching yourself. I was wondering whether it's a nice feeling that, sort of, wakes you up and makes you feel a bit better, maybe a bit less lonely. That type of touching is really private though so I wonder if we can work out some ways that I can help you feel better without the need to touch yourself when other people are around.'

- 'I was thinking about what happened yesterday, when I found you holding Connor down and trying to put your hand in his pants. I was working out how doing that would make sense for you. Do you want to know my idea? I think that for you the feeling of having control, and maybe even scaring people, is really exciting! After all Mike used to make you feel scared and hurt you by putting his penis in your bottom; that must have been so scary and hurt a lot! Nobody seemed to care when that happened to you and so nobody really helped you to understand that it was a really scary thing! I want to help you to understand all those things and make sure that you know how important your feelings and other people's feelings are and so you don't feel like you want to hold Connor down.'

Replacements for sexualised behaviour

Sexualised behaviour in developmentally traumatised children is invariably indicative of an unmet emotional need. Therefore once the underlying need has been understood, carers can apply the strategies that are relevant to the need(s) in both responsive and preventative ways. The preceding chapters have contained details of strategies (detailed specifically below) that are useful for dealing with sexualised behaviour and the unmet needs that cause it.

Replacements for intimacy-seeking sexualised behaviour
In cases where a need for intimacy is identified as the trigger for sexualised behaviour the following strategies from Chapter 3 can be useful:

- attentive nurture (Box 3.8)
- attachment time menu (Box 3.11)
- traffic light system (Box 3.12).

Replacements for control-seeking sexualised behaviour
When it is a need for control that triggers sexualised behaviour the following strategies from Chapter 7 can be useful:

- allowing control (Box 7.4)
- contained control (Figure 7.3).

Replacements for regulation-seeking sexualised behaviour
In situations where emotional regulation can be understood as the cause of sexualised behaviour then strategies from Chapters 3 and 4 can often be useful:

- attentive nurture (Box 3.8)
- attachment time menu (Box 3.11)
- traffic light system (Box 3.12)
- rhythmical calming (Box 4.8).

Box 9.6 Things to remember about sexualised behaviour
Understanding sexualised behaviour

- There are many different types of sexualised behaviour and many different meanings given to the term.
- The nature of the developmental trauma that a child has experienced will in some way show itself in the nature of the sexualised behaviour that a child displays.
- If it is likely that any illegal behaviour has taken place then it is important for the legal process that witness statements are taken before these therapeutic conversations.
- It is useful to share information about sexualised behaviour with relevant professionals.

- It is necessary to acknowledge the details of sexualised behaviour in order to understand the reasons for it, as that detail will help to reveal the unmet need(s) that drive the behaviour.
- In broad terms sexualised behaviour can be grouped into three categories:
  - sexualised behaviour towards adults
  - sexualised behaviour towards other children
  - sexualised behaviour alone (but being indiscriminate about who witnesses the behaviour).
- Sexualised behaviour can arise from a range of experiences in infancy. It is not simply the result of sexual abuse but such behaviour can also be caused by intrusive care, physical abuse, domestic violence and neglect.
- Applying reward-punishment thinking in dealing with sexualised behaviour in children can result in increasing the levels of shame, which may have the effect of hiding rather than reducing the behaviour. This in turn may result in an increased, rather than decreased, risk of the behaviour being repeated.

Understanding what to do

- EBM for carers:
  - Responsive strategies:
    - A good understanding for a carer of what their own emotional reactions are likely to be can help them to be calmer and less judgemental of their own reactions.
    - Carers should not try to deny or mask their feelings but understand them and work with them.
    - Carers should try to acknowledge the details of the 'sexualised behaviour' in order to understand its cause.
- Preventative strategies:
    - It is useful for carers to prepare for their reactions to sexualised behaviour.
    - Carers should take some time to practise and get comfortable with the sexualised language that they may have to use to discuss the behaviour with their child.
- EBM for children:
  - Responsive strategies:
    - It is important for carers to avoid shaming their child about the behaviour.
    - Responsive empathic commentary.
    - Substitutes for sexualised behaviour.

- ◦ Preventative strategies:
  - ▪ Preventative empathic commentary.
  - ▪ Replacements for sexualised behaviour.
  - ▪ Replacements for intimacy-seeking sexualised behaviour:
    - ▫ attentive nurture (Box 3.8)
    - ▫ attachment time menu (Box 3.11)
    - ▫ traffic light system (Box 3.12).
  - ▪ Replacements for control-seeking sexualised behaviour:
    - ▫ allowing control (Box 7.4)
    - ▫ contained control (Figure 7.3).
  - ▪ Replacements for regulation-seeking sexualised behaviour:
    - ▫ attentive nurture (Box 3.8)
    - ▫ attachment time menu (Box 3.11)
    - ▫ traffic light system (Box 3.12)
    - ▫ rhythmical calming (Box 4.8).

CHAPTER 10

Difficult Sibling Relationships

It is very common for there to be conflict between siblings who have lived together through abuse and/or neglect. This conflict can take many forms. It often presents as extreme sibling rivalry but there can also be a problem with dominant/passive and authoritarian/acquiescent sibling roles.

This chapter will cover competitiveness, general rivalry and apparent jealousy between siblings who have grown up together. It will also explore the relationships and roles between siblings that frequently develop as a result of adaptive responses to early abusive and/or neglectful relational environments.

Examples

Kevin and Lameece

I have talked about one of Kevin's rage outbursts in Chapter 4. Kevin, aged ten, and Lameece, aged six, were part of a sibling group of four. Kevin was the oldest child and Lameece was the youngest and the only girl. All four children lived with their adoptive parents, Sue and Joe.

Prior to being removed from their birth family the children had been exposed to physical abuse and frequent episodes of extremely violent domestic abuse of their mother at the hands of their father. Due to the emotional vulnerability and mental health difficulties of their mother, Kevin had also frequently acted as parent and protector to her and his siblings.

Kevin told me about an occasion when his father, who didn't live with the family, had visited the house whilst drunk. Kevin explained that his father was going after his mother but because Lameece was in his way he had picked her up and thrown her to the ground, causing Lameece to knock her head on the edge of a glass coffee table. Kevin painted me a vivid picture of the cut on Lameece's head, the way she was screaming with pain and fear, and the amount of blood that came from her wound.

Kevin explained how he had shouted to his other siblings to stay in their rooms and followed his father in an attempt to protect his mother. He recalled standing at the entrance to his mother's bedroom, watching his father kicking and punching his mother until she 'went quiet'. Kevin then hid until his father left the house.

Kevin explained how he then woke his mother and tried to talk to her as she curled into a ball and wept. He described the amount of blood and that he tried talking to his mother and cuddling her but said that she 'wouldn't talk to me'.

Kevin also described another occasion on which he had seen his mother leave the house late one night taking a large kitchen knife with her. Kevin believed that she was going to kill herself. He followed her, taking the house keys and locking the door behind him because 'the kids were in bed so I didn't want anyone getting in'. After looking for his mother for some time, Kevin found her in an alleyway sat on the floor crying. Kevin managed to talk his mother into coming back into the house and took the knife away from her.

It was documented that Kevin provided his siblings with food, often when there was nothing in the house, and made sure they went to bed and got up for school. The children's school attendance was high. Kevin left his birth family when he was seven years old.

Kevin's adoptive parents were concerned because Kevin dominated his siblings, especially Lameece. He would frequently order her around 'like she was his slave' and threaten her with violence if she did not do what he told her to. The children's adoptive parents explained that Kevin was even able to intimidate her with a look and gave the example of a look that he had given Lameece at the dinner table, which, they said, caused her to stop eating and give him the food that was left on her plate.

Sue and Joe were, understandably, very concerned. They felt that they were being subtly undermined by Kevin and that the younger children were more willing to follow instructions from Kevin than from them. They had worked hard in their attempts to instil confidence in the younger siblings to stand up to Kevin and were vigilant of his behaviour and reprimanded him when he 'bullied' them. They sent him to his room and removed his games console. None of these things had been very effective and the parents said that Kevin was becoming more 'crafty' about his 'bullying'.

Sue and Joe also mentioned that Lameece would frequently speak to them using a 'baby voice' that they could barely understand. This seemed to happen most frequently when Lameece was asking them for something.

Simrita and Gurpreet

Simrita and Gurpreet were siblings who were in a short-term foster placement with their carer Parminder. Simrita, 13, and Gurpreet, nine, had lived at home with their mother and father until six months prior to my involvement. The children had come into the care of the local authority having been neglected by their parents. The alarm had been raised by Gurpreet's school, who noted that he had always been 'a bit grubby', his clothes were dirty and he was frequently smelly. He suffered with enuresis and the school reported that he was coming into school in urine-soaked clothes and other children had started to pick on him as a result.

Simrita's teachers reported that she was a quiet, withdrawn girl with few friends. They also reported that she did not pose any behavioural challenges at school.

Parminder reported that, individually, the children were both settling in well and that whilst they were quite shy, they were also polite and seemingly happy children. However, Parminder explained that every time they were together they fought and argued over even the smallest issues. Parminder described that at meal times Simrita and Gurpreet would examine each other's plates to make sure that they had exactly the same amount of food. If they hadn't then they would argue with each other, push and jostle, try to take each other's food, and become furious with Parminder.

Parminder also described that both children were very possessive of her and would stick to her like glue whenever anybody else was around, particularly the other sibling or Parminder's daughter. Simrita, in particular, would become very angry with Parminder, and she would scream and shout at her carer and brother. On one occasion Simrita physically pulled her brother off the sofa on to the floor because he was sitting next to Parminder when she wanted to.

Parminder said that she felt as if her house had become like a war zone and that it was seriously impacting upon her own daughter (aged 19) and husband.

Typical strategies

Carers can be invited into a particular way of responding to the difficult relationships of siblings, which can influence the strategies that they use (Box 10.1). In the case of sibling relationships that are marked by significant controlling, dominating behaviour it may also be useful to look at Chapter 7.

Box 10.1 Relationship replication: difficult sibling relationships
Birth family experience

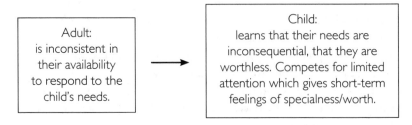

The parent is inconsistent in their availability to respond to the child's needs. They are preoccupied with other things and unable to tune into and respond to the needs of their child. The child learns that their needs and feelings are inconsequential and that their feelings will be ignored leading to the development of a 'not special' and 'worthless' self-image. In the presence of other people attention must be fought for. The victor gains some short-term feelings of specialness/worth.

Foster/Adoptive family experience

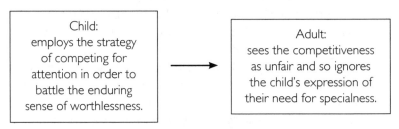

The child cannot tolerate others getting attention when they are not, as this indicates that they have more worth/are more special. Consequently the child competes for the attention. The carer interprets the child's competitiveness as dominating others, being unfair and demanding so ignores the child's 'excessive' attempts to get attention. The carer is therefore not responsive to the child's communications of need and responds to them inconsistently.

Although this example focuses on attention this can be substituted for other sibling rivalries.

SUMMARY: The inconsistent and misattuned parenting leads the child to compete for feelings of 'specialness'. The child has unconsciously invited their carer to ignore their attempts to feel special and worthwhile. The carer has accepted the invitation.

It is quite typical when there are dominant/passive dynamics in play between siblings to punish the child who is dominating, as demonstrated in the case of Kevin and Lameece, above. It is also common for carers to work hard to help the 'passive' child to increase their confidence and ability to assert themselves.

In cases in which there is a particularly dominant 'parentified' child, carers often feel quite undermined and superfluous. These feelings can lead carers to take an imposing approach to their care and being tempted to wrestle for the control of their family (see Chapter 7 for a discussion of how to deal with children who need to control).

Invariably intense sibling competitiveness, as with Simrita and Gurpreet, causes conflict between both children and their carer. This may exhaust the carer and reduce the empathy and positive bonding in the family relationships.

In sibling groups where there is competitiveness, carers frequently attempt to keep the children apart as much as possible in order to avoid conflict and competitiveness. Carers usually follow a principle of fairness and try to ensure that the children are treated equally. Conversely some carers take the view that competitive children have not had enough experience of losing, that is, that they have been allowed to win and perhaps spoilt in this regard. Consequently these carers present their child with more experiences of losing in the hope that this will teach them to be a gracious loser and this reduce their competitiveness.

Making sense of difficult sibling relationships

The elements of the 'child's mind' part of the EBM model (Figure 10.1) that are most pertinent when seeking to understand the difficult sibling relationships of developmentally traumatised children are the need to relate, hard-wired survival strategies, the effects of experience on brain and biology, trauma memory and shame (in bold).

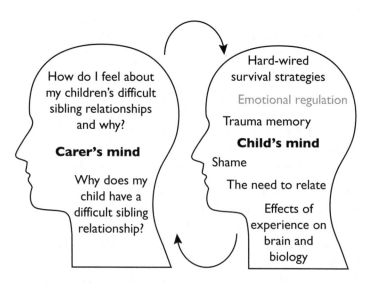

Figure 10.1 EBM model of difficult sibling relationships

Dominant/Passive roles

The need to relate

As I have discussed in previous chapters a baby's need to relate means that they develop their character in response to the way they are treated by their primary carer(s). Children who have lived with the need to have emotional and/or physical responsibility for their own well-being and/or responsibility for the well-being of others (parents and/or siblings) also attempt to retain tight control of their environment (see Chapter 7 for more detail). This can translate into extremely dominant roles in relation to their siblings.

In the case of Kevin and Lameece it was very valuable for his siblings that Kevin was in control. He appears to have been the only person around who had any instinct to protect them from the violence of their father or the abandonment of their mother.

Kevin had become a 'parentified' child, that is, he had been required to take too much adult responsibility for his survival and that of his siblings. Children like Kevin pay the extraordinarily high price of cripplingly burdensome responsibility but, in order to perform their 'parental' role, without adult maturity they need to have uncompromising and dictatorial control.

In Lameece's case she had learned that her needs are best served by doing as Kevin tells her. Such children have sacrificed their autonomy and desire to protest in order to survive, and so it is unfair to expect them to assert themselves and take responsibility for their own behaviour and decisions. Their submissive 'baby' role has, after all, helped to keep them safe.

Whilst these roles are defaults for such children and, as such, offer them a certain amount of comfort, they are likely also to feel a huge amount of simultaneous rage due to the high doses of fear that they have experienced. They are therefore left in the intolerable position of being irresistibly drawn to their dominant/passive roles whilst these roles create in them simultaneous satisfaction, comfort, rage and fear.

Hard-wired survival strategies and effects of experience on brain and biology

In times of extreme stress and fear such as the example of Kevin and Lameece's experience, the brain defaults to survival mode and behaviour is primarily directed by safety-seeking and avoidance of danger. When this experience is played out repeatedly in infancy the strategy becomes hard-wired and may become the default position for dealing with similar relationships.

Kevin's need to dominate his sister, even in an apparently safe environment, was driven by his default of anger and fear. Lameece's acquiescence to Kevin's intimidation was partly a sensible reaction to his very real potential to hurt her. However, it was also her own hard-wired default way of dealing with distress and having her emotion regulated; for many children in this situation the experience of relinquishing control can be physiologically calming.

Trauma memory

The need to dominate, take responsibility and/or take control, in parentified children, or the need to submit and/or acquiesce in 'passive' children, can be a reaction to a trauma memory. The triggered memory may be of any number of traumatic feelings from fear, stress, emotional dysregulation to simply a sensory or emotional memory of stressful relationship circumstances. The mere presence of siblings with whom a child has developed such survival strategies may, in fact, be enough to trigger the dominance/passivity instinct in children.

Shame

Any attempt to reprimand a child that enacts their trauma-generated survival strategy with reward-punishment thinking will result in an increase in shame; something the child is ill equipped to cope with. This is because the child is, in effect, being reprimanded for using their survival strategies and is unlikely to have had access to the compassion in infancy necessary to tolerate shame.

Competitiveness

The need to relate and shame

Children learn the ability to tolerate loss and separation through building a trusting relationship and learning in infancy that they are 'special' in the eyes of at least one person.

Rather than competitiveness being due to insufficient experience of losing, the child has already 'lost' too many times in their earliest relationship. Specifically, they have not had a consistent experience of being put first, something that is crucial for infants. Having the experience of being consistently put first in infancy, that is, had their needs responsively and empathically dealt with, enables a child to internalise a feeling of 'specialness,' that is, positive self-esteem.

Competitive children are, in effect, fighting for that dizzying buzz of specialness by being the best or most important in some way. Such children feel the absence of such feelings almost constantly. Competitiveness can, therefore, be seen as attachment-seeking behaviour and so many of the ideas in Chapter 3 will be useful in understanding competitive children.

Hard-wired survival strategies and effects of experience on brain and biology

Competitiveness is a useful strategy for children who have not been afforded enough attuned, sensitive care. Fighting tooth and nail for the attention of someone that they depended upon but who is largely unavailable is a very sensible strategy to have developed. Standing by and watching somebody else getting attention when the child knows that there is a limited amount available is dangerous. A developmentally traumatised child operates on the assumption that if there is attention to be had then they must maximise their opportunity to get it.

Consequences of using reward-punishment thinking with difficult sibling relationships

Siblings who act out dominant/passive roles and siblings who are extremely competitive are often separated as it is frequently assumed that this will stop their behaviour. However, this fails to take into account that experiences in infancy and early childhood are hugely influential in shaping children's brains, personalities and, therefore, how they interact with other people. Consequently, even if children are separated from the sibling with whom they enact their traumatised roles, they will, in all likelihood, take this role into other relationships.

There are cases in which the trauma of the sibling relationship does even greater damage than the child's relationship with the abusive/neglectful parent(s). The stress of the respective roles that siblings take in relation to each other may disrupt their ability to repair their early trauma via a healing relationship with their carer. In such cases, if the trauma cannot be worked through via therapeutic parenting then, separating siblings can be the best option for developmentally traumatised children, in order that children can be therapeutically parented.

When siblings are not separated and attempts are made to change the relationship dynamic between siblings it must be done with mindfulness and empathy for the loss of role and identity that it is likely to cause. These roles and identities are likely to have kept the children safe and so must be treated with respect and empathy.

It is very common for the dominant sibling, in such relationships, to be punished for their survival strategies; after all it is potentially very damaging to the passive sibling. However, the maintenance of such roles is frequently more damaging to the dominant sibling. They are the ones who have placed themselves at risk, taken all of the responsibility, and then are likely to be condemned for this role by adults and wider society. In addition, there is often more of an expectation of change placed on the dominating character rather than the passive sibling.

Attempts to change dominant/domineering behaviour via reward-punishment thinking are likely to fail to deal with the underlying drive, that is, the hard-wired survival strategy. Therefore it is more likely to force the child to become more subversive and deceptive with their behaviour rather than to stop it.

Without empathic approaches taking precedence, reward-punishment strategies may also threaten the child's already fragile self-esteem and identity.

The typical strategies that are used to deal with competitiveness between siblings are to increase the likelihood that the child will lose, or to take a somewhat inflexible approach to equality. The former will almost certainly increase both the child's level of shame and thus their defensive, competitive behaviour. The latter, whilst more likely to succeed, may also mean that the opportunity to instil a sense of 'specialness' is missed.

It is only if blame and judgement can be removed from the understanding of the relationships and that they can be understood as sensible and inevitable survival strategies that we can help each child to step out of their traumatised role.

Empathic behaviour management strategies for difficult sibling relationships

EBM for carers

RESPONSIVE EBM FOR CARERS

It is important for carers to take the opportunity, when siblings are conforming to their traumatised roles, to notice what their own instincts and feelings about the siblings' interactions are. It may be useful for carers to use Box 2.12, in Chapter 2, to help them with this. Carers can use this understanding to help inform them of the buttons that may be pressed by the sibling relationship and thus the feelings that may impact on the way in which the carer deals with the behaviour.

PREVENTATIVE EBM FOR CARERS

In a calm period when carers are not immediately confronted with any challenging sibling dynamics, it is useful for them to take some time to reflect and understand their own feelings and reactions to the children's relationship and behaviour. Box 10.2 may assist carers to explore their experiences and expectations of sibling relationships. Box 10.3 will help carers to explore their own thoughts about the dominant/passive roles that developmentally traumatised children sometimes take.

Box 10.2 Your experiences and expectations of sibling relationships

Carers might like to try the following exercise to explore their thoughts and feelings about how sibling relationships 'should' be.

What is your experience of sibling relationships?

- Do you have brothers and sisters?
- Do you have a relationship with anyone that is like a sibling relationship?
- Do you know, at close quarters, any sibling relationships?
- What was your experience of this relationship in childhood?
- What is your experience of this relationship in adulthood?

Describe this relationship

- Was it positive, negative, mixed?

Think of a memory/an incident that you think represents this relationship in some way.

How did the/your parent(s) behave in relation to this sibling relationship?

Has this relationship shaped your character in any way? If so, how?

Describe the ideal sibling relationship.

Box 10.3 Your experiences and expectations of dominance and passivity in relationships

Carers might like to try the following exercise in order to explore their own thoughts and feelings about dominance and passivity in relationships.

Have you ever felt bullied? If so, describe an incident that caused this feeling.

Have you ever taken more of a backseat in a decision-making process? If so, describe one such incident.

Think of a relationship in which you have been more dominant and describe it.

Think of a relationship in which you have taken more of a backseat and describe it.

How does being in control make you feel?

How does taking a backseat make you feel?

Would you classify yourself as being generally more dominant or passive in relationships?

What are your expectations of gender in relation to dominance and passivity in relationships?

EBM for children

In relation to dominance/passivity roles between siblings it may be useful for carers to take a look at Chapter 7 and the strategies there.

For issues with sibling competitiveness associated with attachment-seeking, Chapter 3 may be useful in order to boost children's sense of specialness and therefore reduce their need to compete.

RESPONSIVE EBM FOR CHILDREN

Empathic commentary

Empathic commentary can be used in the face of both the dominant and passive roles that siblings take and the competitiveness between siblings and sibling figures (Box 10.4).

Box 10.4 Responsive empathic commentary for difficult sibling relationships

The following are statements that carers can try using in response to difficult sibling relationships. These examples and the Golden Rules in Box 3.9, Chapter 3, can be used to help carers to come up with their own.

Dominant/Passive roles commentary

'You two are doing your old role again? Of course you are! You haven't had a chance to grow the trust in me to give up those roles yet. I really want to help you both feel like you can let me be in control and that I'll keep you safe but I know that can't happen yet.'

'Wow, it really feels like you should do what your big sister tells you to do! I can understand that; she was more like a mum than a sister for a long time! I want to try and help you both trust that I can do the mum thing for you both now.'

'You're telling Marc what to do again. I can understand why you do that. You used to have so much responsibility for keeping him safe that it was really important for him to do what you said without questioning you!'

'I can absolutely understand why you behave like that with your brother. It must feel really scary to think about being equals, like you might get treated the same, because in the past that wouldn't have been safe and being in charge is part of who you are! And who you are is lovely!'

Sibling competitiveness commentary

'Winning/getting attention all to yourself feels so lovely doesn't it.'

'Oh no! You feel like you're not getting treated fairly! I'm so sorry, it's a really horrible feeling, I hate it too!'

'You two are fighting over sitting next to me. I know you both want to know that I think you're special.'

'Of course you two are fighting over who's got the most Christmas presents! You have always had to fight to be treated fairly; why on earth would that stop now? It's going to take a lot of time for me to help you to believe that you're both special.'

'It feels so important that you get treated fairly. Of course it does! Everybody wants to be treated fairly! You haven't been treated fairly for so long, since you were both tiny. It's going to take a while before you can relax and really believe that I and other people will want to treat you fairly.'

'You two are really arguing over the TV. I think you both believe that if you don't fight your corner so strongly you'll lose out. No wonder, you had to make sure that Mum looked after you and if you weren't the loudest you might well have missed out to the others!'

Structured games/activities

If the primary goal for children taking part in these habitual roles (either competitiveness or dominance/passivity) is safety and familiarity then the most therapeutic way of responding is to provide them with safety and familiarity via offering them those things through interaction with their carer and facilitating structured activities between the siblings.

Difficult sibling behaviour can be diverted into more positive interaction using the attachment time menu in Chapter 3. This can be used with each child individually or carers can bring them together to have a different, pleasurable experience of each other. The best way to do this, whilst maintaining some control over their interactions, is for carers and the siblings to get involved in structured games and activities. These can be any board games, card games, cooking, etc. The main criteria for these activities are that there is a clear structure, there is fun to be had and carer and child do it together, that is, a carer and the children with the difficult relationship.

The carer's role in these activities is to make each child feel as special as possible whilst they are interacting with their carer and with each other. It's important that carers step out of their 'referee' mode and deal with each attempt to compete and/or to fall into old roles with another injection of specialness for the child who is attempting to make them referee. This may sound simple but it is likely to be thoroughly exhausting. As a result carers may wish to place a predefined time limit on the activity, for example, until the cake is made, or for one hour.

Preventative EBM for children

Preventative empathic commentary

These techniques can be useful in order for carers to assist their child in understanding the child's unconscious motivations that lie behind the difficulties in their sibling relationship(s) (Box 10.5). This information can be useful in developing a platform from which to move towards a more rewarding relationship in the future.

Box 10.5 Preventative empathic commentary for difficult sibling relationships

The following are statements that carers can use in order to try to prevent difficult sibling relationships. These examples and the Golden Rules in Box 3.9, Chapter 3, can be used in order to assist the carer to come up with their own.

Dominant/Passive roles commentary

'I've noticed that sometimes you end up letting Craig take all the responsibility for your decisions. I think I understand why though, want to hear what I think? I think that in the past, when you lived with Mum, Craig had to look after you when Mum couldn't. I think you never really learned how to make your own decisions and deal with responsibility. It's no wonder that it's difficult now!'

'I was thinking about your roles, when you tell Jenny what to do and maybe even threaten to hit her if she doesn't do it. It's easy to feel like I should tell you off for that but maybe actually it's the way you and Jenny have needed to be in the past! After all if Jenny didn't do what you said when Dad was around she would have got really hurt! It must have been so difficult to deal with being responsible for Jenny, Josh, Freya and yourself! That's too much for a child to have to deal with! It's not been fair for you! No wonder it's been hard to adjust to a home where you haven't got those responsibilities and where grown-ups expect you not to take control of your brother and sisters, that's a huge change!'

'I think that you all get into this pattern as a result of living at home with Mum and Dad. Are you interested in knowing why I think that? I think that someone had to be in charge and the others had to do as they were told because that was the only way that any of the children would get looked after! Craig tried his hardest to look after you even though he was far too young to know how and you, Josh and Freya had to fall in line or they wouldn't get any food and might have got hurt!'

'Thank goodness you were around, Craig! The other kids would have been lost without you. We just need to find a way to help you feel that you don't have to take control now and that you can enjoy having all the lovely parts of being looked after by an adult who cares about you and keeps you safe.'

Sibling competitiveness commentary

'When you both compete for my attention I think it's because you feel that there's not enough to go around. That was your experience of Mum and Dad after all! I want to try to give you both lots of love and attention.'

'I think that you both feel as if you have to win to feel that you're the best or the most special. Children usually learn that they are special in the eyes of their parents when they're tiny babies but I think you missed out on that because Mum was so poorly and couldn't make you feel like that.'

'I think I need to work harder at making you two feel more special.'

'Making sure that you both get the same amount of food is really important to you. I think that's because you want to be treated the same and maybe you expect that I won't care enough about you to do that. After all, no one in the past has made sure that you were treated well or fairly, so why on earth wouldn't you worry that I'll do the same! It makes absolute sense!'

Identifying old roles
When things are calm it may be useful for carers to spend some time with their child thinking about the role that the child takes. Empathic commentary statements can be used to help children to understand that their carer is not judging the role(s) that they take and that the carer has some good ideas about why they take the roles that they do (Box 10.6).

It is best to use this strategy with all of the fostered/adopted children in the household as their relationship dynamics will operate in relation to each other rather than independently.

Box 10.6 Identifying old roles

Carers might like to go through this worksheet with their children to try to understand what roles the children and their siblings were invited to take in the past.

Who was in charge at your mum and dad's home? Who was the boss?

Who was usually in charge out of all the children? (if not already answered with a child's name)

What does the person in charge have to do? What's their job?

What do the people who are not in charge have to do? What's their job?

What would have happened if the person in charge wasn't there? Why did they have to do this job?

What would happen if the people who weren't in charge weren't there? Why did they have to do this job?

What were the good things about the old role/job that you had to do?

What were the bad things about the old role/job that you had to do?

Does it ever feel like you have to do that job/play that role here?

Does it ever feel like any of the other brothers and sisters have to do their old job/play their old role here?

Building preferred roles

To change children's roles in relation to one another carers can try to help them to identify what is different, in their new home, from how things were in their previous/birth families.

The exercise in Box 10.7 focuses upon children's *thoughts*, therefore it may help them to try new roles. However, they will not necessarily change their *feelings* about the situation and therefore the role that they feel compelled to take. The change in feelings can be approached with exercises and experiences which focus upon enabling the child to build trust with their carer and allowing them to experience positive feelings in their new roles.

Box 10.7 Building new sibling roles

Carers can use this worksheet with their children in order to talk with their child about their roles that might be more useful for the child and their siblings in their new home.

- Who has the responsibility for looking after children in our house?
- Who has the responsibility for making children feel special and loved in our house?
- What does it feel like to think about changing your role?
- What could your new job/role be?
- How can we make sure that you don't have to have all those bad feelings in your new role?
- How can we make sure that you get the good feelings of your role/job without having to do your old job?
- What will we do if the old role/job kicks in even when you don't want it to? What can I do? What can you do?

It is important for carers to make sure that their child's adoption of the 'new role' doesn't become a matter of discipline or willpower. The feelings that will make this new role possible, safe and attractive will be produced in the child by using empathy and building a non-judgemental, trusting carer-child relationship. There is likely to be a significant sense of loss when a role is changed. It is important for carers to hold on to the idea that some elements of their child's previous role will be fine to keep, as it already forms part of the child's character and identity.

Box 10.8 Things to remember about difficult sibling relationships
Understanding difficult sibling relationships

- Carers may find that Chapters 3 and 7 may also be useful in dealing with difficult sibling relationships.
- Conflict and difficulty between siblings who have lived together through traumatic experiences are very common.
- Two common sibling relationship issues are competitiveness and dominant/passive roles.

- In the case of the latter it is tempting to discipline the dominant sibling.
- It is important to take the value judgement out of parenting such children and understand the reasons and functions of the respective roles. Often 'dominant' children will have made huge sacrifices in order to protect and 'parent' their siblings.
- In the case of sibling competitiveness and difficulty with not being 'the best', children are usually fighting an internal battle against their history of battling for fair treatment and 'specialness'.
- Competitive behaviour has often developed as an adaptive strategy to a parenting environment in which there is not enough care to go around and where what there is must be fought over.
- Responding to difficult sibling relationships with reward-punishment thinking can lead to an increase in the child's levels of shame and promote defensive, deceptive behaviour in order to maintain the behaviour.
- Reward-punishment strategies can also lead to a loss of role and threaten the already fragile identity of developmentally traumatised children.

Understanding what to do

- EBM carers:
  - Responsive strategies:
    - A good understanding for a carer of what their own emotional reactions are likely to be can help them to be calmer and less judgemental of their own reactions.
    - Carers should not try to deny or mask their feelings but understand them and work with them.
  - Preventative strategies:
    - Your experiences and expectations of sibling relationships.
    - Your experiences and expectations of dominance and passivity in relationships.
- EBM for children:
  - Responsive strategies:
    - Empathic commentary.
    - Structured games/activities.
  - Preventative strategies:
    - Empathic commentary.
    - Identifying old roles.
    - Building preferred roles.

Neuroscience Glossary

Cortisol sometimes known as the 'stress hormone', a *neurochemical* produced by the adrenal gland in times of stress

Diencephalon and brain stem (reptilian brain)

Epigenetics the way genes change depending on our infant experience

Executive functions see *pre-frontal cortex*

Genetics what is inherited from our parents

Limbic system the second layer of the brain, where humans hold their ideas about relationships and emotional safety

Metabolise cause chemical changes in living cells

Neurochemical a chemical involved in processes in the nervous system

Opioid a chemical that relieves pain

Pre-frontal cortex (neo-mammalian brain) the area directly behind the forehead; it helps us to think about the future, understand cause and effect, have empathy and manage strong impulses and emotions. These sophisticated cognitive abilities are often called *executive functions*.

References

Chapter 1 'I've Tried Everything! Why Isn't It Working?'

Blower, A., Addo, A., Hodgson, J., Lamington, L. and Towlson, K. (2004) Mental health of 'looked after' children: a needs assessment. *Clinical Child Psychology and Psychiatry 9*, 117–129.

Brewin, C.R., Dalgleish, T. and Joseph, S. (1996). A dual representation theory of posttraumatic stress disorder. *Psychological Review 103*, 4, 670–686.

Dimigen, G., Delpriore, C., Butler, S., Evans, S., Furguson, L. and Swan, M. (1999) Psychiatric disorder among children at the time of entering local authority care. *British Medical Journal 319*, 675.

Eccles, J.C. (2005) *Evolution of the Brain*. London: Routledge.

McCann, J.B., James, A., Wilson, S. and Dunn, J. (1996) Prevalence of psychiatric disorders in young people in the care system. *British Medical Journal 313*, 1529–1530.

Meltzer, H., Corbin, T., Gatward, R., Goodman, R. and Ford, T. (2003) *The Mental Health of Young People Looked After by Local Authorities in England: Summary Report*. London: Stationery Office.

Miller, P. (2012) A thing or two about twins. *National Geographic*, January 46–65.

Perry, B. (2011) *Integrating Principles of Neurodevelopment into Clinical Practice: Introductions to the Neurosequential Model of Therapeutics (NMT)*. Conference, Woburn Abbey.

Schore, A.N. (1994) *Affect Regulation and the Origin of the Self*. Hove: Lawrence Erlbaum.

van der Kolk, B.A. (2005) *Developmental Trauma Disorder*. Available at www.traumacenter. org/products/Developmental_Trauma_Disorder.pdf, accessed 4 June 2013.

Chapter 2 The Importance of Carers' Emotions

Beek, M. and Schofield, G. (2006) *Attachment for Foster Care and Adoption: A Training Programme*. London: BAAF.

Chapter 4 The Red Mist

Dejonghe, E.S., Bogat, A., Levendosky, A.A., Von Eye, A. and Davidson, W.S. (2005) Infant exposure to domestic violence predicts heightened sensitivity to adult verbal conflict. *Infant Mental Health 26*, 3, 268–281.

Mason, J.W., Wang, S., Yehuda, R., Riney, S., Charney, D.S. and Southwick, S.M. (2001) Psychogenic lowering of urinary cortisol levels linked to increased emotional numbing and a shame-depressive syndrome in combat-related posttraumatic stress disorder. *Psychosomatic Medicine 63*, 387–401.

McBurnett, K., Lahey, B.B., Rathouz, P.J. and Loeber, R. (2000) Low salivary cortisol and persistent aggression in boys referred for disruptive behavior. *Archives of General Psychiatry 57*, 38–43.

Chapter 5 The Girl in a Bubble

Cicchetti, D. (1994) Development and self-regulatory structures of the mind. *Development and Psychopathology 6*, 533–549.

Flack, W.F., Litz, B.T., Hsieh, F.Y., Kaloupek, D.G. and Keane, T.M. (2000) Predictors of emotional numbing, revisited: a replication and extension. *Journal of Traumatic Stress 13*, 611–618.

Perry, B.D. (1997) Incubated in terror: neurodevelopmental factors in the 'cycle of violence'. In J. Osofsky (ed.). *Children, Youth and Violence: The Search for Solutions.* New York: Guilford Press.

Schore, A.N. (2001) The effects of early relational trauma on right brain development, affect regulation, and infant mental health. *Infant Mental Health Journal 22*, 201–269.

Chapter 6 The High-Energy Child

Lewis, M. and Ramsay, D. (1995) Stability and change in cortisol and behavioural response to stress during the first 18 months of life. *Developmental Psychobiology 28*, 8, 419–428.

Index